Sean McManus

Web Design

7th edition

In easy steps is an imprint of In Easy Steps Limited
16 Hamilton Terrace · Holly Walk · Leamington Spa
Warwickshire · United Kingdom · CV32 4LY
www.ineasysteps.com

Seventh Edition

In Easy Steps Limited supports The Forest Stewardship Council (FSC),
the leading international forest certification organization. All our titles
that are printed on Greenpeace approved FSC certified paper carry the
FSC logo.

MIX
Paper from
responsible sources
FSC® C020837

Printed and bound in the United Kingdom

ISBN 978-1-84078-985-0

Contents

7 CSS: Giving your pages some style   105

1 The web design challenge

Web design is the art of creating websites that are attractive and easy to use. But it's complicated by the different browsers and devices visitors have. Learn about the principles that will keep everyone happy.

Hot tip

You can find resources for this book at www.ineasysteps.com or www.sean.co.uk

The goal of this book

The most exciting thing about the internet is not the way it's transformed virtually every industry, nor the way it's enabled us all to be better informed about the world and more in touch with our family and friends than ever before.

It's the fact that anyone can join in. If you've got something to share, the world is waiting.

You don't need anyone's permission to set up a website. You don't even need that much money: you can host a site for less than $10 or £10 a month, including a free domain name. Of course, you might want to pay more for hosting with advanced features, such as more storage or databases.

If you're promoting your business, you might prefer to commission professional designers, and maybe even pay someone to help promote your site. If you're doing it all yourself, it will cost less but you'll need to spend more time on it.

In this book, I'll teach you the key principles of web design, which is the art and science of building effective and attractive websites. This book will introduce you to the key technologies of the web, and the design principles that underpin successful sites.

Whether you're a budding designer who plans to build your own site, or you just want to be able to talk to professional designers in their own language, this book will give you an understanding of how websites are designed so that you can make the right decisions in launching your own site. You'll also be able to build your own simple website using HTML and CSS. When you find useful code snippets and templates online, you'll know how to edit them and integrate them into your website correctly.

I won't claim that you'll be a website design professional by the end of this book. The best websites are built using a combination of technical and artistic skill, and a solid understanding of how people use the internet. It takes time to develop these. Above all, it takes practice to learn how to make the most of the technologies the web offers.

But, as the philosopher said, every journey begins with a single step. And this book will ensure you set off in the right direction, with robust knowledge of the technologies and techniques that will deliver the best experience for your visitors.

The diversity of devices

One of the skills a web designer needs is the ability to put themselves into the shoes of the website visitor. Web designers have to think about what their visitors know, what they will expect the website to do, and how they will expect it to work.

The most basic part of this is understanding the range of different devices that people might use to view your website.

These include:

- A desktop computer or laptop.
- An Android phone, iPhone or other handheld device.
- A tablet device, such as an iPad.
- A games console, such as the PlayStation or Xbox.
- A smart TV.
- A screen reader, which reads web pages aloud to blind people.
- A refreshable Braille display, which a blind person can run their fingers along to read the website content.

When we use the word "design", we tend to think of something visual. But, in its purest sense, a website isn't necessarily a visual medium. Somebody using a screen reader might experience it as a stream of spoken text.

While you do need your website to look appealing, it's a mistake to think that you can (or should) focus purely on the look of a website. Some of the most important work in web design goes on behind the scenes, where the visitors can't see it. It's about adding information so that people can use your web page easily even if their device doesn't support all the features available on a desktop computer.

The challenge of web design is to create a site that is engaging and easy to use, whatever is used to access it. Visitors want the flexibility to use whichever device they prefer. Sometimes they will switch devices, using a desktop during their lunch break at work and a mobile on the way home, for example. All they care about is whether the site works or not. It's your job to make sure it does.

Websites can be viewed using a number of different devices. Shown above, from the top: Apple iPhone; Xbox games console; Alva refreshable Braille display.

How devices affect design

Different devices have different capabilities, and this should inform the decisions you make while designing your website. For example:

Hot tip

Web browsers are mostly free of charge, so why not download a few of the popular ones so that you can try them out? You'll get a taste of how they differ from your browser of choice, and can use them for testing your website design as it evolves.

- There might be no support for pictures (or "graphics") on the device. A screen reader and Braille display can't show images, and some browsers (including Google Chrome) enable users to switch them off to speed up their browsing.

- There might be no conventional keyboard. It puts everyone off if they have to type in lots of information to use a website, but those who have to use a virtual keyboard on their touchscreen might be especially deterred.

- Animation might not be supported or usable. Non-visual devices (such as screen readers) can't render it. Users of smaller screens risk missing something important if the screen display is changing out of their view. Users with poor vision can use screen magnifiers to massively enlarge a small part of the screen. If people are zoomed in on one part of the page, they can't see any updates you make to a different part of it.

- There might be no mouse. Some users struggle to use a mouse because of physical impairment, and some devices (including games consoles and laptops) don't have a mouse. If you demand precise use of a mouse, you might lose visitors.

- There is a wide range of screen sizes. Even on a desktop computer, people will have different-sized monitors and will open the browser window to different widths, depending on what else they're doing at the same time as web browsing. Designs that look good on a small screen won't necessarily look good on a huge one. A Buy button might be easily visible at a glance on a large display, but out of view on a small screen. Designers tend to have large monitors, but they shouldn't forget that most of their audience have to settle for smaller screens.

- A screen reader user can't get a quick overview of what's on the page by skim-reading it – while a screen is two-dimensional, a screen reader has a one-dimensional interface: a stream of audio reading the web page aloud. Using clear headings helps screen reader users navigate the page quickly.

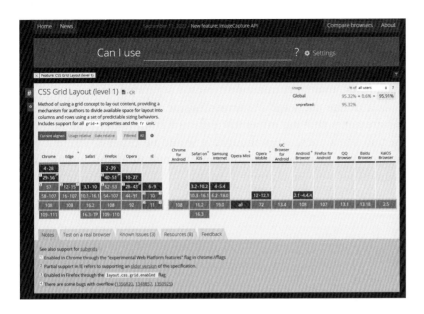

Left: The website **caniuse.com** enables you to search for an HTML or CSS feature and see which browsers support it. Hover over a browser version to see more information about its level of support for the feature and the browser's market share.

The web browser challenge

As well as the differences in hardware used to visit websites, people often have a choice over which software they use.

The most popular web browser is Google Chrome. While estimates of Chrome's market share vary, they're typically between 60% and 70%. Safari is the next most popular browser, largely because it's the default on Apple's mobile devices. Other popular browsers include Microsoft Edge, Firefox and Opera.

The variety of browsers is another reason website design is a challenge: web designers have to build sites that work with a wide range of different browsers, and each browser has its own quirks. In recent years, a lot of progress has been made in standardization. However, new features are sometimes available earlier in some browsers than others, and some people still use old browser versions that don't support the latest features.

You can choose to ignore browser versions with a small market share, but are you willing to turn away those customers? The cheapest way to acquire customers is to serve people who are already visiting your website.

It's better to create a site that works for everyone, and let your visitors decide how they want to experience it.

Hot tip

Use your web analytics software to identify the most popular browsers among people who visit your website. Bear in mind, though, that anyone who can't use your website easily might just leave. See Chapter 14 for more on analytics.

Hot tip

Take every opportunity to try out your website on unfamiliar devices. It's impractical for most people to own every device available, but if you come across one in a shop or at a friend's house, don't miss the chance to see how your site performs.

Degrading gracefully

You might be thinking that the solution is to create a different website for all the different user groups you have. You're not the first to think of this.

In the past, many organizations created separate websites for mobile device users and for screen reader users. These users have requirements that are extremely different from the typical PC user, so many companies thought it would be easier to make a separate site for them than to reconcile their needs with those of mainstream website visitors.

There were several problems with this approach:

● It was time-consuming and costly to maintain separate sites.

● The accessible sites, in particular, often became neglected and out of date. Visitors couldn't access the latest news, although it was available on the main site. The organization's attempt to look after blind visitors by specifically catering for their needs ultimately resulted in them being discriminated against.

● Some screen reader users felt they were missing out because the organization had stripped out all the visual content. Although they couldn't see the content, they were still interested in what was in it and what its message was.

One site for all

Today, it's not necessary to create a separate website for specific audiences. There are too many different devices and configurations for you to cater for them all anyway.

Instead, you should aim to create a single website design that adapts to the device that is viewing it. Many organizations use a "mobile first" strategy, building a phone-friendly website and adding enhancements for larger screens.

The site should degrade gracefully. That means that it can still be used if particular features aren't available on the visitor's device or browser. For example, if somebody can't see a photo, you should provide text that explains its content. If the web browser doesn't support content created using JavaScript, visitors should still be able to navigate the site and use the rest of its content.

A well-designed website will work on any device and web browser.

Understanding accessibility

Accessibility is all about making sure your website can be used easily by everybody. When people talk about accessibility, they often think of blind people using screen readers. But it's not just about those who use completely different technologies to visit your website.

There are lots of people who have more subtle needs that you can help or hinder through the way you design your website. A lot of these people wouldn't consider themselves to have any special needs at all. They'd just find your website hard to use, and give up. For example:

- Can somebody who is color blind understand the availability of tickets, or is it shown only as different-colored blobs?

- Can somebody who has impaired vision increase the font on your web page so that it's easier to read?

- If somebody can't use the mouse, can they navigate your site using the keyboard?

- Can a visitor with impaired hearing get the same information that you've included in an audio file?

- Can somebody with a mental impairment understand your content, or is it too jargony and long-winded?

Most professional website designers today understand the importance of accessibility, but it's the least visible aspect of a website design project, so it can be overlooked. Much of the important work is to do with how a website is coded, and when you visit it using a conventional desktop PC, you can't easily tell whether it's been well designed for other devices or not.

Accessible websites tend to be easier for everybody to use. They work well on mobile devices, and are easier for search engines to index, too. If you need to convince colleagues of the importance of accessibility, you could argue that you want to reach as many customers as possible, or could point out that your business might contravene disability discrimination laws if you don't.

Most websites strive for accessibility because they want to be as inclusive as possible, though. It's not hard to make most websites accessible, and it doesn't cost any more, as long as you plan to make your site accessible from the start.

If you outsource your design, take particular care to make sure the designers are creating an accessible design. If you're never asked to provide any alternative text for images, ask yourself whether they're making it up, or not bothering with it at all.

Try navigating the web by keyboard for yourself, especially your own site when it's ready for testing. In Google Chrome, click a web page and then use the **Tab** key to move through the links. Press **Enter** to visit a link and **Alt + Left arrow** to go back. Use the **Up** and **Down arrow** keys to scroll the page.

Top accessibility principles

I'll share some tips for making your site accessible when we look at HTML later, but there are some basic principles that can go a long way toward making your site easy to use.

1 Provide alternative text for anything that isn't text, such as an image or video. This does not necessarily appear on screen. When you add an image to a web page, for example, you can also provide alternative text that is only presented to the user if the image isn't available.

Make sure your alternative text conveys the same information that it is replacing, but keep it brief. You can say "close up of clock tower", or "the gold detailing of Big Ben shines on a sunny day". Ask yourself what the purpose of the image is, and try to articulate that. You don't have to mention the blue skies or where the big hand is pointing unless it's important.

2 Make sure that your site still works when JavaScript is switched off. When this is impossible, provide the same information in text form on an accessible web page.

3 If users have to respond within a certain time limit, make sure that they are warned and have enough time to request more time, if they need it. Give users controls to start and stop content that moves or updates itself.

4 Use clear and consistent navigation. Make sure that users can easily understand where each link will take them, and give each page a unique title that describes its purpose.

5 Make sure the website can be used with the keyboard, and that users can see which link or element they are focused on.

6 Make it easy to skip straight to the content. If your web page has a long list of links or header information, provide a link that enables people to jump straight to where the article starts. This is particularly important for screen reader users.

Hot tip

Don't provide alternative text for purely decorative images. Make these background images so that assistive technology can ignore them.

7 Don't open pop-up windows, or change the window the user is in, without warning. This is confusing if you can't see the screen, and it stops the **Back** button working, the most important navigational tool on the internet.

8 Use the simplest language appropriate for your site's subject matter. Complicated language is harder to understand, especially if you can't easily flick your eyes back to the previous line for a refresher on what it said.

9 Give users control over how they view your content. Make sure your site works, for example, if people enlarge the default text size in their browser.

10 Make sure that any information conveyed by color can also be understood in other ways. For example, it's okay to use different colors to draw attention to different icons, but you might also make them different shapes or put them in different columns to indicate their meaning.

11 Make sure there is enough contrast in the foreground and background colors you choose for everything to be legible on a black and white screen.

12 Avoid overcomplicated page layouts. If there are too many different sections or boxes, it can be overwhelming for visitors to try to navigate.

13 Test whether your website code has any errors in it. Desktop browsers can be quite forgiving, but assistive technology might struggle to understand your web page if it includes technical errors in the HTML or CSS code.

14 Use the accessibility features available in your HTML code to help people navigate tables and forms. They enable you to provide a context that might otherwise be communicated by the position of things on the screen.

15 Don't use a picture of text unless it's essential. It's a good way to show a company logo, for example. But don't create an image for a paragraph of text just because you like a particular font.

Hot tip

For detailed guidance, see the Web Content Accessibility Guidelines (WCAG) published by web standards body W3C (**www.w3.org/ TR/WCAG22/**). Section 508 (**www.section508. gov**) outlines accessibility requirements for US government agencies, and includes good advice for all websites.

17

Hot tip

There are several automated accessibility checkers online, including Wave (**http:// wave.webaim.org/**). This tests your website against the WCAG guidelines. It helps to identify problems, but accessibility is about whether people can use your site, not whether it appears to tick a particular box. Use your own judgment and feedback from users, too.

Your website will also include a file for each image, and might also include files for audio recordings, videos and downloadable files like brochures in the printer-friendly PDF format.

MySQL is the name of the database software most often used with PHP. Hosting companies sometimes charge a bit more for servers that support PHP and MySQL, but can usually help you to set up the database. You can find lots of free PHP scripts you can install on your server to offer features like forums.

Introducing key technologies

A website is made up of several different coding languages. Here's a summary of the role they play in your website:

HTML

HTML is the main language used for writing web pages. When somebody downloads one of your web pages, the first thing they are sent is an HTML file. HTML describes the structure of your text content, and tells the web browser where it can find the other files for the web page, including its images and CSS files.

CSS

CSS is used for the design and layout of your web page. It contains instructions for colors, fonts and layout.

JavaScript

JavaScript enables you to update your web page after it has downloaded, and to respond to user actions on it. Some people have written sophisticated games using JavaScript, but it's typically used for simple effects like refreshing the screen with the latest news. JavaScript is often used to check that a form has been completed correctly and provide immediate feedback. Not all devices support JavaScript, so you need to ensure that your site (especially its navigation) also works without it.

Server scripting languages (PHP/MySQL)

There are a number of different server scripting languages, and they tend to go through fashionable phases. The most popular one today is PHP, but others include ASP. These languages enable you to write programs that run on the server so that web pages can be customized for each visitor. This is particularly useful if the site needs to offer personalized content, such as a social networking site that serves a different homepage to each person depending on who their friends are.

Server-side scripting languages are also used for sites with lots of pages. Their content can be stored in a database, and when somebody wants to look at it, the program on the server makes the web page HTML and sends it out. It saves you having to maintain hundreds of web pages, because you can just take care of one template, the scripting program, and the database of content. We don't have space to cover scripting languages in this book, but Chapter 11 covers content management systems (CMSs), which also enable you to create a database-driven website.

DIY or outsource?

Should you design your site yourself or pay somebody else to do it for you? It depends on what you want to achieve with your website design project.

The strengths of DIY

Creating your own website can be an extremely satisfying creative project. People build websites for the same reason they write novels and sing songs: it's fun, and it's rewarding to increase your expertise over time. Building websites has an added dimension because what you make can be easily found by others, so you can get feedback. It's also a cost-effective approach, compared to hiring a team of professionals.

If you want to build your own website, you can take one of two paths. Firstly, you can learn how HTML and CSS work and code your site by hand. These technologies aren't too hard to learn, and this book includes a quick tour around their most important features to get you started. Hand coding your site gives you maximum control and flexibility.

Once you know how to create websites, you could buy a template and adapt it to accelerate your web design process.

Alternatively, you could use a visual design package. These enable you to build a website in the same way you might make a newsletter with a word processor. They make it much easier to get started with website design, although it can take a lot of effort to build something impressive.

Outsourcing your design

Working with a web design firm is likely to lead to more professional-looking results first time. You can benefit from the firm's experience of designing perhaps hundreds of websites. You can focus on your content and the site's purpose and don't have to worry too much about technical details.

That said, it's still *your* website, and you need to take responsibility for managing the designers. You need to understand enough about web design to know whether their proposals are a good idea or not, and what the technical limitations might be on any designs they propose.

You might also want to learn enough HTML and CSS to be able to edit the design after the project has ended.

If you commission somebody else to build your website, make sure you have the ability to update it easily later.

19

Make sure you plan enough time for the designers to do a good job on your website. Design is a process, with designers suggesting ideas and you providing feedback until you reach the design you want.

How to set up your website

Now that you understand the design challenge, you're ready to take it on! Here is an outline of the process, although your own project might include extra steps, such as getting the CEO to approve the content:

1 **Planning.** Time invested in planning at the start will avoid rework later. In particular, a clear understanding of the site's purpose should inform the whole process.

2 **Content creation.** You need to write your text and gather your pictures so that the website can be designed to present them in the best way.

3 **Web design.** This involves many small steps. You'll need to structure your content, and design how it is presented. You also need to think about how people will move between different parts of your website. You can commission a web design firm, or you can learn the technologies to design it yourself.

4 **Testing.** To make sure your design works, you need to test it at regular intervals. Design is often an experimental process, with the designer implementing an idea, testing it with prospective site visitors, and using the feedback to refine the design.

5 **Launching the website.** To make your website available to the public, you need to copy it onto a web server, which will send the web pages to your site visitors over the internet. You will need to rent web server space from a hosting company.

6 **Promoting the website.** Attract visitors by making it easy for people to find your site through search engines, adverts and links.

7 **Measuring your success.** Find out how well your site is fulfilling its purpose, and use that information to refine it.

2 Planning your website

Before you design your site, you need to think about its goals, competition and audience; how you will organize its content; and how visitors will interact with it. You should also research web design firms, if you want to use one.

The purpose of your website

It might be tempting to dive straight in and start designing your website, but before you do anything, you need to stop and think. Why are you building a website in the first place? What do you want it to achieve?

The answers to those questions will have an impact on the way you design the site, the features you build into it, and the content you use. In fact, they should have an influence on every part of the project. Everything you do will either be working toward or away from those goals.

Think of the benefits your new website will bring to you and to your visitors. Here are some of the things that a website could help you to do:

- **Build new relationships.** Whether you're looking for customers, investors, fans for your band, or just want to connect with peers who share your interests, a website can help you to attract them from all over the world.

- **Enhance your reputation and profile.** If you want to be known as an expert, then sharing articles or videos that demonstrate your expertise can help. If you're creative, then sharing your music, photos, videos or stories can help you to solicit feedback and build interest in your ideas.

- **Sell, sell, sell!** Of course, you can use the web to make it easier for people from all over the world to buy from you. For digital content, such as music, you can even make it possible for the product to be delivered without human intervention.

- **Improve customer service.** If you have an existing business, you might be able to make it easier for customers to deal with you by publishing manuals and tutorials online. You could take customer enquiries, too, and structure the form so that you capture all the information needed to resolve the query first time. Using the web, any business, no matter how small, can offer some degree of customer service round the clock.

- **Educate.** Whether you want to help the market understand your latest invention or just want to help others learn a hobby, tutorials are among the most sought-after content on the web.

Beware

Don't confuse your website purpose with your website content. A site's purpose shouldn't be, for example, to share photos or to put the company brochure online. That's just another way of saying what content you plan to use.

Hot tip

Think about how you will measure success. Will it be the number of customers, volume of sales, number of comments or subscribers, number of people recommending your content on social networking sites, or something else?

- **Entertain.** Internet users love fun sites, and the web is the ideal medium for sharing short games, films and songs.

- **Create a community.** People like to socialize with and seek advice from others who share their interests online, and many successful websites exist primarily to bring people together. Many of the biggest websites today have been built on the idea of community and of creating new ways for people to communicate.

- **Create new services.** The lines between the website, the product, and the manufacturing process are often blurred. Vistaprint (**www.vistaprint.com**), for example, enables people to design their own business cards, calendars and T-shirts online, which are then professionally printed and delivered by mail. Some websites charge readers a subscription, so the website content is itself the product.

- **Make money.** You might make money by placing advertising against your website content, selling products, or cutting your costs if you already have a conventional business. This can be a strong motivator to build a website, but take care that you don't undermine the end user's experience. You might make more money by plastering adverts everywhere, but you risk driving visitors away.

There are lots of other things a website could help you with, and you might well find that you want to do more than one of the above. The important thing is that you understand why you're building a site. Otherwise, you might get to the end of your design project and find your site doesn't help you at all.

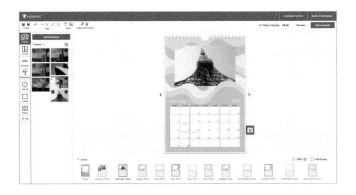

Hot tip

The web can be a relatively cheap way to test new product ideas and to communicate with customers, so you can often afford to be a bit more experimental online than you might be in an offline business.

Hot tip

Google's AdSense (www.google.com/adsense) enables you to host adverts on your website and get paid. Your income will depend on how many people click on the adverts, which will, in turn, depend on how many people visit your site.

Left: Vistaprint enables you to customize calendars, business cards and T-shirts online.

23

How will you compete?

With a website, the competition is only one click away. When people see your site in search engine listings, they'll see your direct competitors at the same time. When they see a link to your site, it will almost certainly be among many other links. If you advertise your site on another site, you need to compete for attention with the content people chose to see in the first place. What do you offer that's special enough to entice visitors to your site?

Companies often talk about having a "unique selling proposition" (or USP), which is a fancy way of saying what differentiates them from the competition. You need to think in terms of how your website benefits the visitor. What do you do better than all the hundreds of similar sites out there? It's easier to compete if you can, in some way, be unique.

To carry out your market research, follow these steps:

1. When looking for potential competitors, think broadly. Search the web for names of products, people, places and benefits. For example, if you're building a site for a book shop, search for the names of authors and books, the subject area of a book you sell (such as "learn web design"), your town, plus the phrase "book shop" (and "bookshop" too).

2. What kinds of expectations do these websites set? Think about the information and features that customers are used to seeing on websites like yours.

3. What kinds of content do these websites post? Is it mainly promotional, or do they also post tutorials and other articles? Do they use video, audio or photos creatively?

4. How do these websites talk to their visitors? Is the tone formal or friendly?

5. Can you learn from their customer feedback? Is there a forum where you can see what customers discuss? If customers can leave reviews, what do they like most?

Don't forget

Your competition online might be very different from your real-world competition, if you have a business. For example, you might be competing with independent review sites and amateur blogs online. People researching the products you sell might well end up at these sites instead of your online shop.

Understanding your visitors

As well as researching the competition, it's important to have a good understanding of who your website visitors, or customers, will be. You can't create a site that pleases everyone, so you need to focus on the preferences of those you most want to reach.

Try to understand, for example:

- Are they mainly one gender, or are they likely to be a reasonably even mixture?

- What stage of life are they at? Are they children, or are they grown up with children of their own? Do they study or work? Are they senior citizens? The kind of design that appeals will vary greatly by age and background.

- How much disposable income could they spend with you? How sensitive are they to pricing?

- What are they interested in outside of your website? Can you use any ideas from popular culture or literature that might appeal to them?

- How comfortable are they using the internet? How much knowledge can you assume they have about how websites usually work?

- Where do they live? Are they mostly in your country, or will you also have readers from abroad, reading in a foreign language?

- What kind of device will they use to view your site? The latest trendy mobile device, or a beaten-up old computer?

Hot tip

Once your site is up and running, you can learn a lot about visitors by studying your web analytics. For now, think about your ideal visitors, and research the visitors of competitive sites.

Left: Lots of data is available online. At the YouGov website (**yougov.co.uk**), for example, you can look up a brand or interest and see what else its fans like. You can also see their gender, political and age profile.

Creating a sitemap

One of the challenges of creating your website is to organize your content into meaningful sections. What those sections are will depend on the content of your site, and its purpose, but you could carve your site up into:

● Product types, brand names or product names.

● Audiences, such as buyers and sellers.

● Areas of interest, such as environmental news, technology news and book reviews.

● Classes of content, such as stories, games and videos.

● Activities that site visitors can undertake, such as shopping, reviewing or downloading.

The important thing is that the grouping makes sense to your prospective visitors. It should be possible for visitors to find what they need without having to click between all the different sections to hunt for it. If somebody was reading a page about a camera you sell, they wouldn't expect to have to go to two different sections to read reviews of it and see videos about it. In that case, it would make more sense to organize all that content into a single section dedicated to that camera.

If your content is diverse, or you have a large catalog of products, you can use subcategories, too. You could have a top category of cameras, with subcategories for consumer cameras, semi-professional cameras and professional cameras. Or you might have a main category for cameras, which contains subcategories for different brands.

Thinking like a customer

It's easy to forget that customers don't use the jargon you do, and might not be familiar with your site's content. A lot of businesses create sites that closely mirror how their company divisions are organized, but that often makes no sense at all to outsiders. Visitors don't know where to start looking for what they need.

Try to use simple language to define each section. If you can't do that, then consider reorganizing the sections or creating subcategories to reduce complexity.

Hot tip

The sitemap doesn't need to include every link on your site, nor every piece of content. It's just an overview of the main paths people can take to get between the main content areas. Don't feel you have to represent every single page.

As well as defining how the content is split up, you need to have a sense of how the sections are related to each other: what content deserves to be on the homepage, for example, and what content can be pushed a few clicks away from it.

Developers often create a sitemap, which represents the way the site sections are linked to each other, similar to the way that a roadmap might represent connected neighborhoods.

It doesn't really matter how you make this. One approach is to write the section names on sticky notes, and then arrange them into a sequence that makes sense, drawing lines between them to represent connections and hierarchy. You can easily add, remove and reposition sections by moving the sticky notes around.

Below you can see two different sitemaps for a band website, mostly based on the same content, but placing a different emphasis. The first, for example, has the shop as a major section. The second pushes free music to the homepage and sells through the Music section.

Hot tip

You can create a page on your website that has links to all the pages on it, and this is often called a sitemap, too. It can help people if they get lost or can't find something on your site. Search engines can also use it to discover all your website's content.

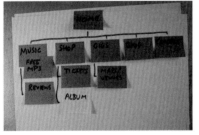
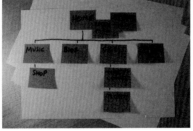

Asking your customers to help

To help you work out the categories that products belong to, you can ask some of your customers or target audience to carry out a card sorting exercise. To do that, you give them a set of cards with the names of the different content areas or pages on them. They then organize them into groups that make sense to them, suggesting some category names too. You could also ask them how they think the categories should relate to each other. Make sure you use a representative sample of potential customers if you carry out this exercise. Don't rely too much on one person's view.

Hot tip

There is another meaning for sitemap. You can create a specially formatted sitemap file to help Google index your website. Google usually indexes a site by following the links between its pages. If there are more than 500 pages, or not all pages are linked to others, a sitemap helps Google find everything. This sitemap is never seen by site visitors. It's just for search engines.

27

Planning interaction

Something that has a huge impact on a site's development is the degree of interactivity it enables. Every site allows people to navigate it using links, of course, and most enable the use of contact forms and search boxes.

Hot tip

Don't overcomplicate your site. If all you want to do is publish information, it's okay to have a simple website with basic interaction.

Some websites, though, enable much more sophisticated interactions and become almost indistinguishable from software. Social media sites are as fully featured as any email program, for example. Adobe has online photo-editing software, including Adobe Photoshop Express Editor (**www.photoshop.com/tools**):

Think about how you want people to interact with your content. For example, do you want them to be able to vote or comment on their favorite pages? Do you want to include an interactive tutorial that explains how your technology works? What about enabling people to customize content and download it, like the photo-editing example above? Do you want people to be able to connect with their friends and share information with them?

In short: what kind of experience do you want your website visitor to have? And what will you empower them to do?

In many web design projects, the degree and type of interaction determines the complexity and cost. Animation requires more specialist design skills, for example, and any website that involves storing data from visitors will need software to be installed on the server. In many cases, that software will need to be written especially for the website, which can be expensive.

Hosting your website

Your website is made up of files that are stored on a computer that people can access over the internet. This computer is known as a web server. These files will include the text, graphics and layout instructions for your website, among other things.

When somebody wants to see one of your web pages, their browser will request it over the internet. The server will send them back the files they need for that web page, and the browser will combine them all and present them to the user.

Few people who run a website ever see their server. They work with a hosting company, which rents them a server or, more usually, just some space on a shared server. These servers are kept in data centers with high availability and dedicated technical teams to respond to any faults.

When you are choosing a hosting solution, look for the following:

- **Storage space.** This is how much space all your website files occupy on disk. If you will allow users to contribute content that is stored on your server, then you need to count this, too. The amount of storage space is one of the big differences between differently priced hosting offerings.

- **Bandwidth.** This is how much data you can send over the internet each month. This is a function of how many visitors you have, how many pages they look at, and how big the files are on your website. It's common for hosting deals to include unlimited bandwidth today.

- **Secure Sockets Layer (SSL) certificate.** This encrypts the traffic between the user's device and your website, protecting the visitor's privacy. Google prioritizes secure sites in search rankings, and Google Chrome warns users a site is not secure if it doesn't use SSL.

- **WordPress.** Many hosts offer a simple installation process for the popular content management system (CMS) WordPress.

- **Email.** Hosting packages can also include email addresses at the same domain as your website, simplifying communications with your visitors.

- **Databases.** If you're building a site that uses databases, for example using MySQL, you'll need a hosting package that includes databases.

Hot tip

Usually, you can start small and upgrade as the scope and popularity of your site grows. Sometimes, you will need to start with a more expensive hosting package, because you want to use technologies that have special hosting requirements, such as PHP, and these might cost more. It's worth researching hosting early so that you can launch as soon as your site is ready.

Hot tip

Well-established hosting companies include Ionos (www.ionos.com) and GoDaddy (www.godaddy.com). If you work with a web design company, they will usually take care of the hosting for you.

Why domain names matter

Each web page on the internet has a unique address that is known as its URL (short for Uniform Resource Locator) – for example: **www.sean.co.uk/books/web-design-in-easy-steps/index.html**

This URL is broken down into several different parts:

- **The domain name:** This is the address of the website, and is used to find the server that hosts the files. All the files on the same website will start with the same domain name. In this example, the domain name is **sean.co.uk**. The **.co.uk** part is the domain extension, and it describes what kind of website this is (a UK-based commercial one).

- **The folders:** These explain where the required file is on the server. In our example, the folders are **/books/web-design-in-easy-steps/**, and it means the file is inside the "web-design-in-easy-steps" folder, which is, itself, inside the "**books**" folder. This is similar to the way that folders are sometimes described on a Windows PC.

- **The filename:** This is the specific web page – in this case, **index.html**, which is one of the traditional names for the start page in any particular section of the website. The **.html** at the end is the file extension, and it explains that this is a HTML file. Image files will have a different extension, such as **.jpg**.

It is possible to launch a website without having your own domain name, but I wouldn't recommend it. Some years ago, lots of musicians built websites that were all hosted by MP3.com and that all shared the **MP3.com** domain name. When that business was sold on, all those pages were shut. Bands lost the audience they had spent years building up, and all the incoming links they had. Fans lost contact with the bands because their bookmarks no longer worked. If your site is hosted on somebody else's domain name, then that organization has absolute control over your website.

Owning your domain name gives you independence. If your hosting company messes you around, you can go to a different one, and take your domain name with you. Visitors can still find you, and all your incoming links will continue to work. Domain names can cost less than $10 or £10 a year, and are one of the best investments you can make in your website.

Hot tip

To work out whether you own your domain name, ask yourself whether you own the bit immediately before the domain extension. For example, I don't own **sean.example.com**, because I don't own example.com.

Hot tip

Once you have your hosting and domain name, you can publish a simple holding page to tell people what you will launch there and when. Include some search engine keywords (see Chapter 13) so that search engines can start building a profile of your domain.

8 domain name buying tips

Here are some top tips for buying your domain name:

1 Any reputable hosting company can tell you whether a domain is already registered or not.

2 It's usually easier and cheaper to buy your domain name from your hosting company.

3 Keep it short. Your visitors will often have to type it in.

4 Make it memorable and avoid things that can't be spelled easily or would need to be spelled out on the phone.

5 Your domain extension can help you tell visitors what kind of site you have. There are extensions for different countries and types of sites – for example: **.co.uk** for UK companies, **.me.uk** for personal websites, **.ca** for Canadian websites, **.mobi** for mobile sites, **.biz** for businesses. You can use **.com**, **.info**, **.net** and **.org** for anything. You can invent creative domains using the extensions of foreign countries, such as **.tv** (Tuvalu) or **.me** (Montenegro).

6 Don't try to buy all the different variants of your domain name. You'll go both mad and broke. There are way too many. It might be worth buying a couple of domains for key markets you want to work in (such as the **.com** and **.co.uk** variants, if you intend to create different websites for the US and UK). But otherwise, it's best to accept that you can't own every variant.

7 Search engines will consider any keywords in your domain name to be important, but don't overdo it. You could have something like **www.bloggs-bakery.com**, but you wouldn't want to have **www.bloggs-bakery-bread-boston.com**. It makes you look desperate for visitors.

8 As soon as you work out the domain you want, buy it! Others might be interested in that same domain, and if you snooze, you lose!

Whenever a new extension is announced, there's a rush to register domains. Preregistration with a registrar doesn't guarantee you'll get the domain. It just means your chosen registrar will join the race on your behalf, up against other registrars who might be after the same domains.

Make sure your domain isn't ambiguous. www.goredfoxes.com should be read "Go Red Foxes", the name of an athletics team, not "gored foxes", for example.

Domain name pitfalls

Domain names are valuable assets, so it's important to look after yours. There are several scams involving domain names that you should be aware of, although they are thankfully becoming less common now than they used to be.

Firstly, the renewal date of your domain name is a matter of public record. Rival domain registration companies sometimes phone up or post letters that look like invoices and ask you to renew. While they consider this to be clever marketing, a lot of people think of it as a scam. Many people are tricked into transferring management of their domain name to another company, and even if the site continues to be well hosted, do you want to deal with a company that markets itself like that?

To protect yourself from this scam, know when your domains are due for renewal, and beware of any communications that come too early or from organizations you haven't dealt with before. If you get any paperwork you don't understand, ask your current hosting company or web designers to explain it.

Another scam involves companies phoning you up to try to sell you domain names you don't need. They will often say they have another client who is about to register a domain name that is similar to your company name or existing domain name, but they want to give you first refusal. You can safely ignore this. If the domain name is registered and hosts a competitive website, laws that prevent others from trading on your goodwill protect you. If the domain name is registered and used for an unrelated purpose, it's not doing you any harm. In most cases, it will never be registered, of course, because the client who was about to register the domain is entirely fictional.

You need to take care when you're researching your domain name, too. Some unscrupulous domain registrars will register domains you express an interest in but do not immediately register, in the hope that they can sell them to you at an inflated price later. Only check the availability of your domain name on a reputable hosting company's website. You can also check who owns a website (if anyone) by running a "whois" search at the internet registry for an extension, which is basically the organization in charge of it.

For **.com** and **.co.uk** domains, there's a single tool that checks both at **https://lookup.icann.org/en**

Working with web designers

You can design your website yourself, but many people prefer to work with professional web designers. They bring the experience gained from working on lots of previous projects, and the level of expertise that comes from developing websites full time.

If you decide to work with a web design firm, you still need to understand what makes a website effective, and need to make sure that your site meets your goals. Your designers will bring a lot of creativity and insight to your brief, but you will need to work with them to manage the project successfully.

Choosing a good designer

You can find web design firms through a search engine, through adverts in magazines, or through your local phone book. You can find freelancers worldwide, through sites like Fiverr (**www.fiverr. com**) and Upwork (**www.upwork.com**). Designers often work remotely, without meeting their clients, but you might prefer to work with somebody local.

Take a look at the web designer's own website, as well as those in his or her portfolio. Don't be seduced by flashy graphics, unless they would help you to satisfy your site's purpose. Look at how easy the sites are to use, and how well they meet their objectives. Try resizing the web browser window, navigating by keyboard, and typing nonsense into forms, to see if the site still works. See whether you can find the websites easily using a search engine, and try out the sites on different devices.

Often, the portfolio sites will have been designed with different requirements from your own, but you can learn a lot about a design firm by checking how flexible and search-engine friendly their sites are by default.

How web designers charge

Web designers usually quote a fixed fee for the project. This is based on their estimate of how much time it will take them, considering the scope of your project and how easy you will be to work with. If you can reassure them that you will respond promptly to their requests for feedback and input, and supply materials in a form that's ready to go on the website wherever possible, you might be able to save money. There can also be regular maintenance costs, which are a good investment if you think you might need the designer's help to keep the site running.

Some web design firms specialize in creating sites for particular market sectors. Try searching for something like "web design law firm" to see if there are any companies who specialize in your line of business.

Make sure you have a formal contract with your web designer, and that it transfers the copyright of the website design and related materials to you.

...cont'd

Hot tip

A good understanding of web design, gained from reading the rest of this book, will help you to understand and manage your design team.

When to engage your web designers

It can take some time to find designers you trust, so it's a good idea to start looking as soon as possible. However, you should probably wait until your content has been created before you kick off the design project. Otherwise, you run the risk of having to cut your content to fit the design.

Finishing the content first also means you can then focus your attention on the design, which makes it easier for you to provide timely testing and feedback.

How to brief your designers

To get the best results from your web designers, give them the freedom to be creative. If you have a clear vision for your website, by all means share it. But don't dictate the layout, color scheme, navigation, and so on, unless you're certain you've got a better design than they might otherwise have come up with.

Instead, start by sharing those aspects of the site you have already planned. Tell them about the website purpose, and how you plan to differentiate your site from the competition. Provide as much information as you have on your audience and the kinds of devices they might use to view your website. Share your concept of how you want visitors to interact with your website, and send them the content you already have.

If you can provide examples of competitive (or even unrelated) websites that you love and hate, and explain why, that will help the designers gauge your taste.

Designers will often create mock-ups of the design, using an art package like Photoshop at first, so that you can agree on the look and feel of the site before they spend too much time developing web pages. When you have alternative designs to choose from, it's usually okay to mix and match ideas from them. These mock-ups are part of the web design project, and you shouldn't expect designers to speculatively create them for free.

Providing feedback

Keep in touch with your design team and provide timely and regular feedback. Make sure that you thoroughly proofread and test the final web pages. Ultimately, you are responsible for the quality of your own website.

3 Creating effective website content

Once you've planned your site, the next step is to think about its content. You could use text, photos, audio, video, and maps to help get your message across.

Hot tip

Make the most of the content you already have. You might be able to reuse information from brochures, CVs or resumés, and conferences.

Beware

If you publish an email address online, it will attract junk mail (spam). You could register a free email account and use that for web queries, to protect your main address. Alternatively, you could accept queries through a form so that your email address isn't published. You can use a CAPTCHA on the form to stop automated submissions. This is a simple puzzle that requires human intelligence to solve, such as reading some distorted text.

Ideas for content

Before you can consider designing your website, you need to create your content. Doing it the other way around is a bit like designing the packaging before coming up with the product idea: it might work, but you'll probably have to chop a few bits off the product to fit it in the box.

The content you choose to publish will be determined by your site's purpose and the message you want to get across.

Essential content for every website

- **About us/me.** When visitors arrive at your site, they might not know anything about you. Some context about who you are, what you do, and why you're different helps them understand everything else on your site.

- **Contact page.** Even if you're not selling, it's good to have a dialogue with your visitors. You'll be surprised how helpful some visitors can be, telling you about broken links and similar issues. If you are selling, it's essential to reassure customers that they can contact you with any problems.

Content ideas for business sites

- **How to find us.** Make it easy to find your office or shop.

- **Meet the team.** The web can seem impersonal, so put a friendly face on it by introducing your team members.

- **Product and service descriptions and photos.** People won't buy something they can't understand. Be clear about what you offer and why customers should buy from you.

- **Customer service information.** Answer the most frequently asked questions (FAQs) in advance. Customers get an instant answer, and you save the time spent answering personally. Product instructions can be particularly valuable.

- **Customer testimonials.** Ask your existing customers to share their success stories and reviews.

- **Behind the scenes.** Lift the lid on your business with a photo tour of the factory, or an overview of how you work.

- **Presentations.** Share audio, video and/or slides from any talks you deliver. Consider making tutorial videos purely for use on the website.

Content ideas for any website

- **Blog.** Have a regularly updated section where you comment on what's going on in your business, what's in the news, and what you're thinking. Blogs can be opinionated and often encourage readers to leave their comments.

- **What's new.** Keep the website fresh with the latest news in your industry, company or area of interest.

- **Tutorials.** Demonstrate your expertise and draw in new readers with articles that teach people how to fix things, make things or do things.

- **Interviews.** Can you interview an expert in your field and share their wisdom with your site visitors?

- **Calculators and tools.** Can you help people to solve a simple problem? You could incorporate a simple tool like a tax calculator, a picture resizer or dictionary. Ask yourself, what do your customers look for online that you can offer? HSBC (**www.hsbc.co.uk**) has several mortgage calculators to help visitors understand loan applications and repayments:

Consider using a mixture of different formats for your content. Text is ideal for attracting new visitors through search engines, short videos are popular with many people, and some will download a podcast to listen to during their commute.

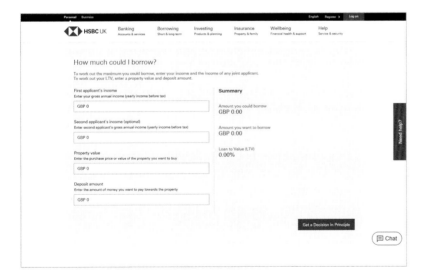

All text and images are automatically protected by copyright. If you didn't create something, make sure you get permission from its creator before using it. Duplicate text can be penalized by search engines, so it pays to invest in creating your own.

- **Games.** Can you get your message across in a game? Games will make your site more entertaining and memorable, and will encourage longer visits.

How web writing differs

Writing for the web is different from writing for printed documents for a few reasons:

- People skim-read web pages, so good use of subheadings and lists is essential for getting your message across.

- Search engines will deliver people to the page that most closely matches their query, not necessarily your homepage. People can start reading at any page on your site, so you can't assume they have read any other pages.

- Sometimes people arrive at your site after following a link they've seen elsewhere. Their expectations of your site will be defined by the text of that link, and any surrounding commentary. This is usually outside of your control.

- People can take any path through your content, following links to explore other sections at any time. You can provide links to background information, so you don't need to clog the story up with excessive detail.

To account for all this, make sure that people can easily work out where they are in your content. To a certain extent, this is a function of how the site and its navigation are designed, but you need to consider it in your content, too. You can't assume that people are reading every word from page one. If you do, you'll confuse visitors, and they'll abandon your site.

Use strong headlines and subheadings to help readers understand the purpose of each chunk of content and how it relates to the rest of the page.

Don't try to railroad readers into following a linear path through your content. Use links to help people find related content that provides additional context. For example, don't tell people all sales are subject to shipping fees and then expect them to hunt for that information. Link it. If you mention other products, then add links to them too. If you give people different paths through your site, they're more likely to spend time exploring it.

You can put a link anywhere in a sentence, and readers will understand it's a path they could take, or they could ignore it. Make sure your link text is descriptive so that people know what they're likely to find if they click it.

Beware

Visitors will use the quality of your writing as an indicator of the quality of your expertise and/or service. It's difficult to proofread and edit your own work, so get a friend (or, ideally, a professional) to check your copy.

Beware

What about PDFs? These are files that preserve the look of a brochure and that you can put on your site for download. If somebody arrives at a PDF file through a link or search engine, though, they won't see your navigation. Their only option is to leave your site again. It's better to adapt the content from the PDF and incorporate it into your web pages properly.

8 top web writing tips

1 **Keep web pages focused.** Cover one topic on each page. It's easier to navigate a series of short pages that include clear links between them than a long page that tries to cover too many diverse subjects.

2 **Put readers first.** Don't bang on about how great you are. Tell readers how they benefit, and make sure you are telling them what they want to know from the very first sentence. Reflect their interests in the headline.

3 **Use a strong headline.** Headlines with verbs (action words) are usually more compelling.

4 **Create a lively pace.** Start a new paragraph for each new idea, and keep paragraphs short. Vary the length of sentences but don't let any go on for too long.

5 **Be consistent.** Format dates and abbreviations consistently, and, where different spellings are possible, pick one and stick with it.

6 **Be specific.** Avoid hype like "award winning" and just say what you've won. Replace "affordable" with the price.

7 **Don't show off.** New writers feel that they have to put on a writerly voice, and end up driving readers away. Keep sentences simple, prefer shorter words and avoid jargon. If you have to use technical terms your readers won't know, define them as you go.

8 **Edit vigorously.** Make every word add meaning. Delete words like "actually", "indeed", "really" and "currently". Look out for phrases that have shorter alternatives. Replace "despite the fact that" with "although", for example. Take care with the passive voice. The active voice is usually simpler. For example: don't say "the mat was sat on by the cat"; do say "the cat sat on the mat".

Read it aloud. If you get out of breath mid-sentence, readers will have forgotten the start of the sentence when they get to the end. If you stumble over tricky phrases, readers will struggle to concentrate.

To help enforce consistency, refer to a journalism style guide. *The Guardian* publishes its guide online for free (https://www.theguardian.com/info/series/guardian-and-observer-style-guide).

Images that work

You can easily shrink digital pictures but can't enlarge them without losing quality, so start with the highest-quality image you can find.

40

Hot tip

Consider the size you will use the image at. Detailed pictures look muddy at smaller sizes. Large pictures can include more detail.

Hot tip

As a minimum, your photos need to be well exposed and in focus. Ideally, they should be well composed, too. Beware of people who have trees growing out of their heads, unsightly shadows and confusing composition.

Web pages without any pictures look bland, but that's no excuse for covering your web page with decorative effects. The number and size of pictures on a website is often the biggest factor in determining how long it takes to download. So, you need to be selective in those you use, and make sure they add maximum value for the visitor.

While it is okay to use some decorative images, the best pictures are those that inform or entertain, and that help you to tell your story. For example:

- Your logo, if you have one.

- Pictures of the products you are selling or writing about.

- Photos of your company's shops or offices, or places you are writing about.

- Photos of yourself, the people on your team, or those you are writing about or interviewing.

- Illustrations that help explain a tutorial, such as an assembly diagram for a computer.

- Cartoon strips, which provide an entertaining way to explain your products or educate your audience.

- Artistic photos, if you built the site to share them.

You will probably find that you already have lots of pictures you can put on your website. You can use photos taken with a digital camera, or can use a scanner to digitize old prints or negatives. You can usually get high-quality product images from the product's manufacturer, too.

Left: Google worked with cartoonist Scott McCloud (**www.scottmccloud.com**) to create a fantastic comic book explaining what was different about the Google Chrome browser (**www.google.com/ googlebooks/chrome/**).

Left: Firebox (**www. firebox.com**) uses several different photos of its products, to give customers a complete view of how the product is used.

Lower down the page, small photos are used to illustrate similar products. When customers click these images, they're taken to the detailed product pages.

Photos also help visitors to navigate their history, providing an easy visual shortcut to pages they've previously visited.

Stock images can look boring and generic. Your site will have more personality if you can create or commission your own images.

Some of the free image sites are sponsored or owned by commercial photo libraries. Some of their images are promoted commercial shots, not free ones.

Using stock photography

If you don't have images of your own, you could license some from a stock photography library. It's sometimes worth paying for a higher-quality image, but several free sites are available:

- CocoMaterial (**cocomaterial.com**), which has illustrations like this astronaut.

- FreeImages (**www.freeimages.com**).

- Unsplash (**unsplash.com**).

- Pixabay (**pixabay.com**).

- Pexels (**www.pexels.com**).

Downloading images

The process for downloading images is similar on many free stock sites. Here's a walkthrough using Unsplash, which I've often used to source high-quality images:

1 In your web browser, visit **www.unsplash.com**

2 Search for a topic or theme you're interested in.

3 Search results may include premium images (labeled Unsplash+), images from commercial stock libraries, or sponsored images provided by brands that include their products in the photos. Most images are free. Scroll to find an image you like and click it.

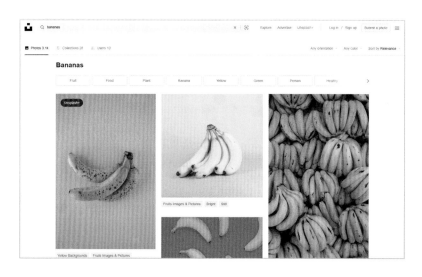

4 The image's detail page has a link to download the image, and information including the photographer's name. Photographers appreciate it when you credit them if you use their images, but it's not required under the Unsplash license. Other licenses may vary.

Hot tip

Above the search results, click **Collections** to find curated collections that are relevant to your search. It's often a shortcut to the best images.

Hot tip

Use the filters above the search results to narrow your results to portrait – or landscape – shaped images, or to find images that use a particular color prominently.

Choosing image formats

As well as the number of images you have, the file format you use for them has a big influence on your website's speed. There are four different image formats that are commonly used in websites, with most websites using a combination of at least two:

- **JPEG.** This format is best for photographs. Depending on the level of compression you use, the image can lose some of its definition. You might see ghosting around the edges of objects, for example. Creating a good JPEG image involves striking a balance between the level of compression and how clear the image is on screen.

- **GIF.** A GIF image can have a maximum of 256 colors, so the format is best used for icons or other illustrations. The compression algorithm is lossless, which means you don't lose any image quality. You can also create animated GIFs, which combine a number of animation frames into a single image file. The browser displays the frames automatically, at your predefined intervals. GIF files can also have a transparent color, which allows the background to show through.

- **PNG.** The PNG format generally offers better compression than GIF and JPEG for icons and other computer art. It also supports more sophisticated transparency, with the ability to have transparent colors that let the background shine through. There is no support in the format for animation.

- **WebP.** This modern format has better compression than JPEG and PNG, so images take up less storage space and download faster. It's not supported on older devices, though, such as iPads that Apple is no longer updating.

Hot tip

Each time the page requests an image file, a script or a style sheet, it has to go back to the server, which causes a delay. CSS sprites combine images into one file. They're beyond the scope of this book, but are worth researching if you use lots of images.

43

Hot tip

Scalable Vector Graphics (SVG) are images created from text code. They're good for icons and illustrations because they can be resized perfectly.

Left: The PNG transparency enables the background to show through the colored dice.

Compressing images

To prepare your images for your website, follow these steps. You can use any image preparation program. If you don't have one, you can use the free IrfanView (**www.irfanview.com**).

1 You can tell the browser to display an image at any size on the screen and it will scale your picture up or down to fill the space. If you use a larger photo than you need, though, you'll slow your website unnecessarily. Photos from digital cameras and other high-quality images will be much bigger than you need for a web page. Your first step, then, should be to resize the pictures so that they are the same size as the largest size you want to display them at. For example, resize your photo from 4272 by 2848 pixels (width by height) to 350 by 233 pixels. Take care to preserve the aspect ratio so that your image is not distorted.

2 Save a copy of the image in your desired file format. For photos or images with lots of color changes in a small space, use JPEG. For graphics, line art, text or logos, use GIF or PNG. Sometimes, you might want to try different formats to see which works best for you.

3 Choose the quality level. You can usually go down to 80% in a JPEG without any noticeable difference. You can often cut the quality much more without significantly hurting the image's appearance.

4 Check the file size and quality are both okay. You can see some extreme examples and a mid-way example below:

Beware

Don't overwrite your original file with a lower-quality version, especially if you're using digital photos from your camera. Create a backup version of your photo first, and then edit that.

Hot tip

Reuse the same images on different web pages. The browser only needs to download them once, so your second page seems much faster.

44

Hot tip

If you're using small preview pictures (thumbnails) to link to larger images, it is acceptable to have a lower picture quality on the thumbnails, as long as the photos can still be identified.

JPEG at 100% quality
File size: 201K

JPEG at 50% quality
File size: 46.5K

JPEG at 10% quality
File size: 27.4K

Adding a video to your site

You can embed videos from YouTube in your site.

1 In your web browser, visit **www.youtube.com**

2 Search for a video that you want to include. You can play the video to find the point where you'd like it to start playing back on your site, if that's not the beginning.

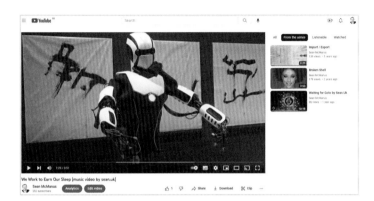

3 Underneath the video, click the **Share** button. When the new pane opens, click the **Embed** button.

4 Choose your options. You can check the box to start the video at the point you paused it (in my case at 1:29).

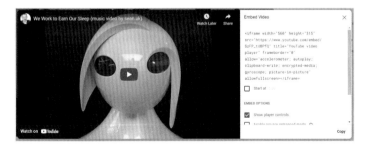

5 The HTML code to embed your video is in the top right. You will paste this into the body of your web page code to make the video play on your site.

In the **Embed** options, you can also enable a **Privacy Enhanced** mode to stop Google tracking your visitors unless they play the video.

You can often embed videos created by others, so it's worth searching YouTube to see if there's something useful to your visitors there.

Chapter 6 covers HTML. You'll learn how to use the embed code later on.

Adding a map to your site

If you have a shop or office that you want people to visit, a map is essential. It's easy to add one using Google Maps:

1 Go to the Google Maps website (**http://maps.google. com**) and search for your address.

2 Use the zoom controls in the bottom right of the map to adjust the view so that you can see as much detail as you want. Click + to zoom in.

Hot tip

Don't forget to include your full address, phone number, and links to relevant public transport websites. Your own directions, mentioning local landmarks, can be helpful too.

3 Click the **Share** button in the left pane. A new box will open. Click **Embed a map**.

4 Choose your map size. It's better to include a large map and make enough room for it than to try to squeeze a small map into a corner of your site. Customers will want to scroll around the map to work out their directions.

Hot tip

You've seen how to embed videos and maps, but you can embed other content too. Getty Images (**www. gettyimages.co.uk**) allows you to embed photo slideshows on non-commercial sites, for example. Look out for other embedding opportunities!

5 Click the **COPY HTML** link. Save this code to paste into the body of your web page later. You'll learn how HTML works in Chapter 6.

4 Layout and design

Your layout needs to communicate order and consistency so that the design looks professional and is easy to use. The fonts, colors and images you choose will combine to create the look and feel of your website.

The layout and design guidelines in this chapter are just that: guidelines. Just take care that you don't break them without thinking about them first.

Don't be afraid to leave some empty space – at the bottom of a column, for example. It gives your design breathing space.

Use whichever tools you find easiest. You could start with pen and paper, use an art package like Adobe Photoshop, or go straight into an HTML prototype.

The role of your design

Now that you've spent some time planning and creating content, it's time to look at the layout and design of your web pages. Your website design needs to achieve the following goals:

- **Encourage engagement.** Your website design needs to inspire visitors to look around your site and spend some time there. It's easy to focus on this aspect of the design, but don't get carried away. Keep the purpose of your site in mind throughout its development; otherwise, you might end up with something that is beautiful, but otherwise useless. Different styles will resonate with different audiences, which is why it's important to understand your target visitors first.

- **Communicate order.** Whether you have five pages or 500, your website design needs to make it easy for people to understand which pages are more important, and which parts of each page are most important.

- **Define the boundaries of the website.** Because people can move between websites so easily, it's important that they understand when this has happened. Using a consistent design across your web pages helps to reassure visitors that they are still on your website. You can create different layouts for different page types (your homepage and product pages are bound to look different, for example), but these should share the same design elements. Avoid using radically different color schemes or graphic styles on different pages, otherwise visitors might think they've gone to a different website. Anything that makes the visitor think about using your website, instead of just getting on with doing so, is a barrier to your site achieving its goals.

- **Feel easy to use.** Your site navigation needs to feel intuitive to visitors so that they can easily find things. They want to spend time using your content, not trying to figure out how to find it. Navigation is so important that Chapter 5 is dedicated to it.

- **Inspire confidence.** If you have a site that visitors consider to be professionally designed, they're more likely to come back or spend money with you. People will (sometimes subconsciously) judge the quality of your expertise or services based on how professional your website looks.

What is your look and feel?

The look and feel of your website is what results from all the decisions you make about its content and design.

It is a combination of:

- The images you use – both the style of your content images and photography, and the choice and arrangement of any decorative images.

- The attitude suggested by your text, and the language it uses.

- The color scheme you have chosen.

- The fonts you use to convey your information and draw attention to important elements.

- The way you arrange elements on the page to accentuate what is important.

You need all these elements to work in harmony. If you were promoting an industrial rock band and had lots of metallic textured images, it would look strange to have a fancy handwritten font or lots of bright kid-friendly colors. Sometimes you can subvert conventional wisdom, but it's usually better to play it safe.

Using design elements consistently sends a signal to your visitors that you've paid attention to the details. It's easy to put things onto a screen. It takes more care to combine them so that they look like they belong together in a single design. Work within a palette of four or five colors (plus shades or tints, as appropriate). Make the spacing between different elements on your web page consistent. Choose one or two fonts and use them throughout.

The rule of thumb is: if things look similar, they should be exactly the same. If they're nearly the same, it just looks sloppy. If you don't want things to look the same, then make them radically different. Leave no doubt that you have deviated from the norm to add contrast or emphasis, or to call attention to something.

When you're developing the elements of your look and feel, keep your intended audience in mind. Think about the kinds of magazines they read, the TV shows they might watch, the films they prefer, and their favorite websites (until yours is built, at least). Use a visual language that will make them feel at home.

Hot tip

Professionals often create the look and feel in an art package, like Photoshop. They make an image of the whole web page. This image can then be sliced up to make the background and foreground images that will form part of the finished website.

The right look and feel

Here are three websites that cater for different audiences. You can see how the design of each matches its visitors' needs:

- The website for UK government services (**www.gov.uk**) is almost text-only, making it extremely fast. The site aims to help readers find what they need quickly, despite the huge amount of content. Concise descriptions guide visitors to the services. At the top of the page are links to popular content and a prominent search box.

- Saga (**www.saga.co.uk**) offers services including insurance and holidays to the over 50s. The homepage uses large promotional images featuring people who are over 50 so that visitors feel like they belong on the site. The experience is like browsing a shop.

- The CBeebies games website is designed for children (**www.bbc.co.uk/cbeebies/games**). It uses text sparingly and keeps the language simple. The navigation uses cartoon icons and the games have audio instructions, so even children who cannot read can use the site. The colors are bold and exciting.

Hot tip

Take a critical look at market-leading sites that cater for a similar audience to yours. It will give you an idea of what others think is a suitable design for your audience and it will also show you what your visitors are used to seeing.

Don't forget

You don't have to use guesswork. You can invite members of your audience to give you feedback on every stage of your design.

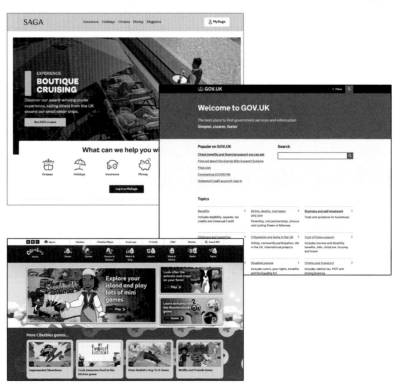

Creating a color scheme

The typical computer can display millions of colors, so how do you choose a handful that work well? The good news is that there are lots of tools that encapsulate the important color design theories, and they're often free. Here's a suggested approach:

1 Open a color scheme tool. Adobe has a free one at **https://color.adobe.com**. You might have one built in to your web design software or image-editing software.

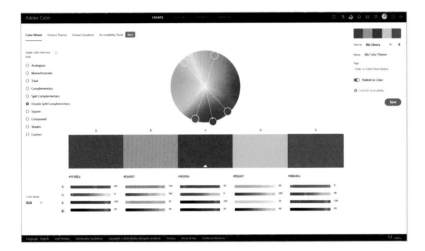

2 Choose your starting color. You usually do this by clicking it on a color wheel. On Adobe's tool, click and drag a circle on the wheel.

3 Choose what type of color scheme you would like to create. A monochromatic scheme uses shades of one color. A complementary scheme uses two colors that are directly opposite each other on the color wheel. A triad uses three colors that are the same distance apart on the wheel. There's also a split complement triad, which uses one color, and the two colors beside its complement on the other side of the wheel. An analogous color scheme uses colors that are next to each other on the color wheel.

4 Note the color numbers in the palette provided. You'll need to put them in your CSS code later.

Most major websites use black text on a white background for their core content. It offers the best contrast, so it's easy to read.

Color wheels encapsulate important design theories. Using a color wheel is the easiest way to create a harmonious color scheme.

The Color Contrast Check tool at **https:// snook.ca/technical/ colour_contrast/ colour.html** checks whether there is enough contrast between your foreground and background colors for easy readability.

Don't get carried away with fancy fonts: remember that the most important thing is that people can comfortably read your message.

52

Hot tip

You can create a distinctive design using unusual fonts for headings and standard device fonts for the main text of the page. Chapter 7 includes a list of safe fonts that are on Windows, Mac and Apple mobile (iOS) devices.

Choosing fonts

The style of text you use on your website has a huge impact on its design. Some fonts are playful, some are business-like; some speak of tradition, while others look futuristic. All this information is conveyed before somebody has even read what the text says.

You should use fonts that convey the personality of your site, where possible, but there are some technical limitations.

The fastest and most efficient solution is to use the fonts installed on the visitor's device. But visitors use a variety of devices, and you don't know for sure which fonts they will have.

You can give the browser a list of font options, so you could request a daring and relatively rare font and give the browser a safe substitute if that font isn't available. You could use a font that comes with Adobe Creative Suite or Microsoft Office, for people who have those packages – for example – and declare a basic font that comes with the operating system, as a back-up.

Harrington

Jokerman

Old English Text

Palace Script

Rage Italic

Ravie

ROSEWOOD STD

Snap ITC

STENCIL STD

If you want to use a font that isn't installed on the visitor's computer, you need to send it over the internet with your web page, which is called embedding it. Not all fonts can be embedded for licensing reasons, and the way to embed fonts varies by browser model and version. Embedding a font increases the download size of a web page, too, slowing it down.

Google Fonts simplifies the process of embedding fonts. It provides an easy way to embed fonts from its own catalog. It sends the smallest possible file, depending on the browser being used, so it helps to improve the user experience.

See Chapter 7 for instructions on adding fonts to your web page.

Planning a responsive design

In the past, organizations often created separate websites for different user groups. In particular, they made text-only websites for those using assistive technology such as screen readers, and they created a separate version of the website for mobile devices.

There were a number of problems with this approach. The accessible sites were often neglected and missed key information. Managing multiple sites was complex, too.

One site for all

Today, you don't have to create separate websites for specific audiences. There are too many different devices and configurations for you to cater for them all anyway. Instead, you should aim to create a single responsive website design that adapts to the device that is viewing it. The site should work well on assistive devices such as screen readers, too.

Analyzing responsive designs

Let's take a look at a responsive design.

1 I'm looking at the website of London's Royal Albert Hall at **www.royalalberthall.com**. If the website has changed since this book went to press or you're curious about what your competitors do, you can use a different site. I've gone to the **Visit Us** page. View the web page in your usual desktop browser.

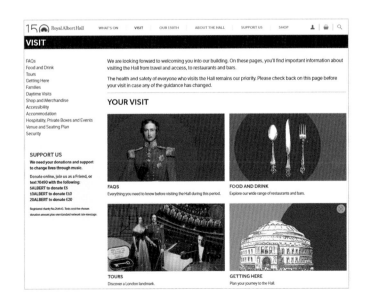

A well-designed website will work on any device and web browser.

Desktop screens are getting bigger, but long lines of text are hard to read. Many sites set a maximum width for the page content, to make sure it's easy to read on even the largest monitors.

...cont'd

2 Drag the right edge of your browser window to make it narrower. As you narrow the window, you'll see the design respond. The site will reflow to use the available space.

3 When the window width reaches a particular point, you might notice new design rules kick in. On the Royal Albert Hall site, for example, the sidebar disappears and the long navigation menu at the top is compressed into a hamburger menu.

A hamburger menu has an icon showing three horizontal lines. It's called that because it looks a bit like two slices of bread with a burger between them. When users click or tap the hamburger icon, the full menu opens.

4 Visit the same site on your mobile device. On the Royal Albert Hall site, much smaller pictures are used, and the text appears beside them instead of underneath them. The site's logo is smaller, too. These screenshots and your own experiments show how a responsive site can tailor the layout, depending on the screen space available.

Using clean alignments

Grids are routinely used for designing print products. Newspapers, for example, use column-based layouts. Sometimes, a picture might span two, three or four columns. But it rarely spans two-and-a-half columns, because that tends to look messy.

Web designers often use a grid to help them position content on screen. Organizing items in boxes supports responsive web design, because the design can change the size and number of boxes on each row, depending on the width of the browser window.

On the **Things to Do in San Francisco** page on the Tripadvisor website (**www.tripadvisor.com/Attractions-g60713-Activities-San_Francisco_California.html**), you can see the grid clearly.

The logo, navbar (see second Hot tip), headings and content boxes all line up with the same invisible left margin. The right edges of content boxes all line up, too. Everything in a row is the same size and aligned vertically.

Each horizontal panel is divided into equal-width content boxes. The number of items in the rows varies, but rows with the same number of items are perfectly aligned with each other.

It's a good idea to use a grid-based layout when you can. Not everything has to sit rigidly on the grid: you can break out of it for emphasis, and to create some pace in the design. But, if nothing lines up, a web page can look amateurish or chaotic.

Hot tip

Even content pages can benefit from a responsive grid layout. You might have a wide box for your article (where space allows) but you can still line it up sharply with your navbar and sidebar.

55

Hot tip

The "navigation bar" or "navbar" is the main group of links for getting around the website (see page 60).

Tips for good alignment

To ensure your web page lines up well, follow these steps:

1 Mark up your content correctly, using the correct HTML tags, to identify a heading or a list item, for example. By default, HTML brings consistency, ensuring that all headlines and bullets line up. You'll learn more about HTML in Chapter 6.

2 Take care when adding spacing using CSS (changing the padding and margin around an element). This can introduce inconsistencies that throw out the natural alignment that HTML gives you. You'll learn how to control spacing using CSS in Chapter 7.

3 Be careful if you're using a visual editing system to build your web pages. They will often let you place content wherever you want on the page, but won't alert you if you're a few pixels out in lining things up. That can lead to designs that look sloppy.

4 It's easier to create a strong alignment, and the impression of good design that goes with it, if you align content with the left or right edge of the page or content box. If you center content, the alignment is harder to see. Centered paragraphs are also harder to read, because the start of each line is harder to find. Newcomers often want to center everything, but you should limit your use of center alignment to a few carefully selected parts of your design.

Right: The inconsistent alignment and center-aligned text look messy.

Far right: The pictures line up with each other, the text above and the company name. The left-aligned main text looks cleaner. The footer is right-aligned with the right margin of the main content box. This is far from a complete web design, but it does show the difference good alignment makes.

Thinking above the fold

As well as column-based layouts, there's another idea the web has borrowed from the newspaper industry: the fold.

When broadsheet newspapers are laid out for sale, they're folded across the middle and only the top half can be seen. The bit that's on show is said to be "above the fold".

Newspapers are designed to have their major headlines and photos in this top half of the page so that people are drawn to them and pick up the paper. The newspaper's branding also appears prominently in this top half so that people can recognize it immediately.

In web design, the term "above the fold" is used to refer to the first screenful of content. It's what people can see without having to scroll the page, so it is their first impression of your website.

It's essential that your website's identity or branding, and its navigation, appears above the fold. By having multiple columns of text, you can also start several different stories above the fold and invite people to click to read more or scroll down the page to finish reading.

Of course, the fold doesn't appear in the same place for everyone. It varies depending on the screen resolution and the device used. So, you need to design your responsive site so that your most important elements are always visible at the top of the page.

People don't always notice the scrollbar, so you need to provide a visual cue to encourage people to scroll down the page. An easy way to do this is to box some of the content, and stagger where the boxes end. People will understand that if they can't see the bottom border of the box, they haven't seen everything.

Hot tip

If a long web page covers lots of different topics, ask yourself whether this should be split into different pages for a better user experience.

Hot tip

People are comfortable with scrolling content. It's okay to have a long web page if the content justifies it. People don't want to read an article split across multiple pages instead.

About us	About us
• Careers • What we do • Contact • Terms • Press • Location	Lorem ipsum dolor sit amet, consectetuer adipiscing elit. Maecenas porttitor congue massa. Fusce posuere, magna sed pulvinar ultricies, purus lectus malesuada libero, sit amet commodo magna eros quis urna.
Other countries • Germany • France • Spain • Italy	Nunc viverra imperdiet enim. Fusce est. Vivamus a tellus. Pellentesque habitant morbi tristique senectus et netus et malesuada fames ac turpis egestas. Proin pharetra nonummy pede. Mauris et orci.

About us	About us
• Careers • What we do • Contact • Terms • Press • Location	Lorem ipsum dolor sit amet, consectetuer adipiscing elit. Maecenas porttitor congue massa. Fusce posuere, magna sed pulvinar ultricies, purus lectus malesuada libero, sit amet commodo magna eros quis urna.
Other countries • Germany • France • Spain • Italy	Nunc viverra imperdiet enim. Fusce est. Vivamus a tellus. Pellentesque habitant morbi tristique senectus et netus et malesuada fames ac turpis egestas. Proin pharetra nonummy pede. Mauris et orci.

Far left: The user has no clue that this page continues below the fold (the red line).

Left: Boxing the left column tells the user the web page continues below the fold, prompting them to scroll.

Make your navigation stand out. Use color, text size or spacing so that it is immediately obvious to visitors. While your text and other content has to be there, people are often just skim-reading it to find the next link they need.

Organizing information

Within each web page, you need to create a hierarchy of information. It needs to be easy for visitors to see what's most important on any given page, and easy for them to skim-read the page to find what they're looking for.

Think of it like a newspaper. The size of the headlines, and their position on the page, tells you a lot about the relative importance of different stories.

Here are some tips for organizing the content on your web page:

● Larger text looks more important than smaller text.

● Things higher up the page tend to be more important than things further down the page.

● Be consistent. If you have 20 different sizes of text, it will be difficult for people to gauge their relative importance. Use up to three different types of headings that are consistently formatted. Using the HTML <h1> to <h3> tags correctly will enforce consistency by default.

● Use bulleted lists and subheadings to structure your content. You can create them using HTML so they're part of the language of navigating the web.

● You can use contrasting color or spacing around elements to call attention to them. Audiobook company Audible (**www.audible.com**), for example, could use a text link to bring people into its free trial process. But it uses a bright orange button with lots of space around it so that there's no mistaking the most important action on this page.

Proximity helps communicate meaning. Don't put half your navigation links on the left and half on the right: they belong together. Keep headings closer to the content they title than the content above.

5 Designing effective navigation

Effective navigation will help your visitors to understand your site structure, to find what they need, and to explore everything your website has to offer. In this chapter, I'll share some guidelines and technical tips to help you create effective navigation.

Good navigation is important for search engines. They will follow the links on your site (or "crawl it"), to discover all your web pages.

Good navigation is invisible. People just use it without noticing it. Only when the navigation is frustrating do people pay it much attention. So, when you're online, think about the navigation you see and what works well. You can use this knowledge to craft your own navigation design.

For retail sites, or sites with a lot of content, a search box is an essential navigation tool.

What is navigation?

Navigation is all about the links you provide to enable people to move between the different parts and pages of your website. Your navigation needs to address four key challenges:

- **Visitors won't know what's on your website unless you tell them.** Entire sections of your site could be overlooked if people don't know they're there.

- **People don't have the patience or commitment to try to work out how to use your website.** They just want to be able to understand it immediately, and want to intuitively know how to get around it. If they can't work out where to find something they want, they'll probably leave your website altogether.

- **People don't know how your website is structured unless you tell them.** They want to feel that they understand where they are in the whole site, not to feel like they're bouncing between pages aimlessly.

- **Visitors will want to take a different path through your website, depending on their interests.** You can't assume or expect that everyone will want to view your web pages in the same order.

It is possible, and desirable, to put links anywhere in your content. If a blog post mentions your latest product, then you should link to it so that people can find out more information easily. Providing links in context at the time people might want them makes it much easier for people to explore your website.

When people think of navigation, though, they usually think of those links that are separated from the content that provide access to everything the site offers. A group of links at the top or the side of the page is often called a "navigation bar", or a "navbar" for short. Because it's separated from the page content, it's easy to spot, and it often uses design elements that draw attention to it.

It's risky to copy another site's navigation, because what works for them won't necessarily work for you. That said, there are certain conventions that you need to take into account. Visitors arrive with some opinions of how a website should work, based on all the other websites they've used. If you can meet their expectations, they'll find it easier to use your site, and you'll find it easier to keep their interest.

Planning desktop navigation

You might think that every website looks different, but if you look closely, you'll see that there's often a lot of overlap in where navigation options are placed on websites. You can use this to your advantage: by borrowing from this consensus, you can make it easier for your visitors to understand how to use your website.

Here's a pattern for your navigation, as seen using a desktop:

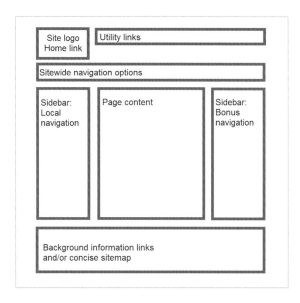

- Your site logo in the top-left corner links to the homepage.

- Your sitewide navigation options are below the logo, or to the side of it. These will be the main links to different sections on your site, such as different types of products. In most sites, these links remain the same across every page of the site. In extremely large sites, these can change depending on the page the visitor is viewing, but they remain the most important links. This navbar should be immediately obvious. Its location helps communicate its role, but you can help it stand out by using larger text, contrasting color or spacing around it.

- Utility links are placed in the top-right corner. These are tools for using the site, so are separated from the content sections or product categories in the sitewide navbar. Utility links might include **My Account**, **Log In**, **Help**, **Customer Service**, **Contact Us**, **Privacy Policy**, and **Search**.

This is only a pattern: it doesn't work for every website. If it doesn't work for yours, don't try to force your website into it.

Some of your web pages might fit equally well in more than one category. **About Us**, for example, could be a utility or a background link for the footer. It's up to you how to categorize links, but it's a good idea to keep similar links together. If you also have links for **Careers** and **Press Releases**, **About Us** belongs with them, wherever they are.

..cont'd

Above: Asda's clothes brand George (**http://direct.asda.com**) matches the pattern without a right sidebar on some of its pages. Utility links include **Track your Order**; the logo links to home; the main navbar shows the different types of clothing; the left sidebar shows relevant links for the current section. At the bottom, visitors can find help with sizes, stores and orders as well as information about the company.

● The left sidebar is used for navigation options that are relevant to the section the visitor is in. For example, if they are in the **Books** section, they might see different genres here.

● The right sidebar can be used for bonus navigation options, such as links to the latest blog comments from visitors.

● The box across the bottom is used for links to background information about the website (such as **About Us**, **Press Releases**, **Investor Information**), and/or to provide a short sitemap with links into the main sections on the site and their most important subsections.

No site exactly matches this pattern, of course. It's a generalization. Many websites will only have one sidebar, either the left or the right one, and some will have none at all. The sidebars often include other content, too, such as advertisements.

Some websites don't have a horizontal navigation bar across the top, and put all their navigation options down the side. But it's a useful crib sheet to help you design your navigation, because it will feel intuitive to visitors.

The pattern also ensures that the most important links have due prominence. All the important navigation options should be immediately obvious when the page loads.

A sitemap at the bottom of the page gives readers somewhere to go when they've finished reading an article and the main navigation has been scrolled off the top of the screen.

Which links belong where depends on your site, but there are a couple of guidelines:

● The shopping cart is often placed in the top-right corner, with the utilities, or on the right of the sitewide navbar.

● A link to the homepage (where present) should be the first item in any navbar.

● The search box can be placed almost anywhere, as long as it's obvious what it is. It's often seen in the top right, in the sitewide navbar, or at the top of the left or right sidebar.

Planning mobile navigation

On mobile devices, there is often not enough screen space to show all the navigation options. The hamburger menu is a popular solution.

The biggest advantage of the hamburger menu is that it makes good use of screen space. It's widely used on websites and apps, so many users are familiar with it.

There are drawbacks, though. Visitors can't see what's in it without tapping to open the menu. Some pages might be overlooked as a result. The additional work involved in finding and opening the menu, even though it's just a tap, risks reducing site interactions compared to a desktop menu where all the options are shown.

A good compromise is to display the main navigation options on the mobile screen and use the hamburger menu for additional options, and especially for pages that users visit less often.

Amazon (below, left) has a horizontally scrolling navbar under its search box and shows the account options and cart in the top right. When the hamburger menu in the top left is tapped, a menu slides out showing popular pages, top departments, and recommended services as shown below, right:

Hot tip

If you're concerned your visitors won't know how to use the menu, you could add the word "Menu" beside the icon to guide them.

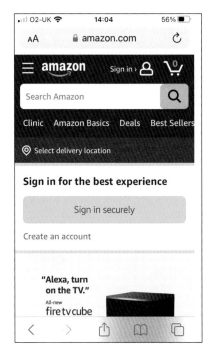

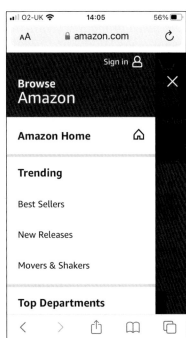

Dropdown menus

A dropdown menu usually opens when somebody puts the mouse over an option on the navbar, or when it is clicked or tapped. It provides immediate access to some of the subpages under that option. If somebody puts the mouse over **About Us** (for example) or taps it, a dropdown menu might appear with options for **Contact Us** and **Recruitment**.

Retailer Target (**www.target.com**), as shown below, uses a dropdown menu. The menu appears to be in front of the site content, so it doesn't take up any additional screen space. When the mouse is clicked out of the menu, it closes again.

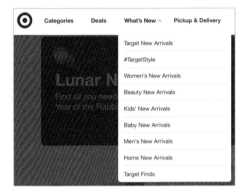

The mega dropdown shows many columns of options when the menu opens. Vistaprint, below, is one example. Mega dropdowns need to be designed carefully to ensure they can be easily scanned by visitors. People skim-read lists vertically, so if you sort the options alphabetically, arrange them in columns and not rows. Within the mega dropdown box, you can use headings for groups of links so that people can find what they want more quickly.

Touchscreen devices can't detect a cursor hovering over a particular place on the screen. The finger is either touching the screen or it isn't. Apple devices use the first touch to trigger the action of a cursor hovering.

64

Don't forget

Dropdown navigation makes good use of limited screen space and helps visitors get to their desired page more quickly.

Grouping options

A navbar's job is to create order and provide direction. That's not always easy: when the site has diverse content or is large, it can be difficult to summarize it through a handful of links.

Take a look at the list of nine links on the left below, for example. It might cover everything that's on the site, but is it easy to use? Not particularly. Long lists of links are hard for people to skim-read, so people have to slow down to use them. That makes the site feel laborious to navigate.

Fixing it is easy. The links can be grouped into three sections: **Shop**, **Free downloads** and **About us**. By putting a small heading above these links, it's easy to see at a glance what's on the site.

Hot tip

Alphabetical sorting is ideal for links where their title is unambiguous, such as the name of a band or TV show. If people might not know what you've called a particular category, or it could be one of several things, alphabetical sorting might not add enough structure to make your list intuitive.

Before grouping	After grouping
• Books	**Shop**
• CDs	○ Books
• Posters	○ CDs
• Wallpapers	○ Posters
• MP3s	**Free downloads**
• Who we are	○ Wallpapers
• Team photos	○ MP3s
• Visiting us	**About us**
• Contact us	○ Who we are
	○ Team photos
	○ Visiting us
	○ Contact us

Whether you are creating vertical navigation or horizontal navigation, the secret to making it work is to group your links in a way that makes intuitive sense to your visitors, and then to communicate that grouping. If you've invested time in planning your sitemap first, you'll find it much easier to do this.

You could use these links with subheadings in the sidebar or the footer, or you could create a horizontal navbar with buttons for **Shop**, **Free Downloads** and **About Us**. When people click those, you could take them to a page with more options for the subcategories, or you could start showing them selected content and provide links to the different subcategories on the left.

Some people say that you should be able to get anywhere on a site within three clicks. It's a helpful guideline, but the most important thing is that people can easily find what they need and feel that they are getting closer to it with every click. Arranging links in easily understood groups helps to achieve that.

Don't forget

Sometimes there are multiple ways to organize navbars. We could have grouped this as **Music** (**CDs**, **MP3s**), **Art** (**Posters**, **Wallpapers**), and **Writing** (**Books**).

Using icons

One way to call attention to important links and information is to create a representative icon for them. Icons can be a useful visual shorthand that enables people to quickly see where they should click or tap, as well as making it easier for them to do so by increasing the size of the link on screen.

There are lots of symbols and metaphors from the real world that are often used on websites. For example:

- From the classroom, a green check mark is often used to indicate that a form field has been completed correctly, with red coloring marking an error.

- The symbols used on a media player's remote control are used for online media: a triangle pointing right represents play, a square means stop, and two triangles go back or forward quickly, depending on the direction they point.

- From the supermarket, a shopping cart is used to represent the page that shows the products the visitor plans to buy.

- From the postal service, an envelope is often used to represent email or contact information.

- Arrows pointing left and right are often used to represent the next or previous stage in a process, respectively.

Lots of professional designers make their icons available for free use on other websites in exchange for a link, or sell a commercial license to those who don't want to link.

Hot tip

Use Google image search to find icon sets. It returns images showing all (or most of) the icons in a set.

Beware

Make sure your icons are big enough to be clear. An icon that is obvious to you, after seeing it throughout the development project, might not be so obvious to the strangers it is there to help.

Right: Iconduck (www. iconduck.com) offers a wide range of free icon sets in diverse styles and colors, as shown by these shopping carts from different icon sets. Try to find a single icon set that contains all the icons you need so that your icons have a consistent style.

The role of the homepage

The homepage has a special role to play in your site's navigation. As the page that people see when they type in your domain name, it's the official first page of your website. Visitors expect it to introduce them to what the site's about and give them some pointers toward content they might want to explore.

If somebody follows a link from another site or search engine, the first page they see might be deep within one of your content sections. If they feel lost, they know they can visit the homepage to reorientate themselves.

There is a simple convention in website design that you should follow to make this easy: put your company or site logo in the top-left corner of the screen, and make it a link to the homepage. It helps to add a **Home** link to your navbar, too, perhaps with an icon of a house to represent it.

Right: The Barnes & Noble homepage (**www.bn.com**) gives people lots of ways in to the site, and leaves no doubt that this is a shop. Shoppers can see special offers, exclusives, and the newest books. The navigation used across the site is introduced at the top of the page, including the search box. The screen space is full of links that entice visitors deeper into the site. Retailers can use their understanding of the customer to tailor the homepage to their interests.

Hot tip

If your site has a lot of content, you might need to have intermediate navigation pages to help people navigate each section. These pages can perform a role similar to what the homepage does for the whole website, introducing the section and enabling people to start exploring its contents. Smaller websites can take people directly from the homepage to the content pages.

Don't forget

Every major section or product category on your website should be represented on the homepage.

..cont'd

Your homepage should include:

- **A short, clear statement explaining what the site is about, if it isn't obvious.** Write a short paragraph near the top of the page. Provide an **About Us** page for the detail.

- **Navigation options that help people find content relevant to them.** Depending on how your site is structured, you could use short snippets of articles with links to full stories, selected products or links to the different categories. While most pages of your site will be dominated by content, the homepage can be almost full of these navigation options.

- **A prominent search box.** Some people might be happy to click around the site exploring it, but many prefer to search. The search box should be near the top of the screen. It's often placed on the right-hand side.

- **The standard navbar.** Because people understand the homepage is different from other pages, you can get away with not having the same layout and navbar. But, if you standardize navigation from the homepage onward, you can start teaching visitors how to navigate your site from the very first page.

Fiction writers are always advised to "show, not tell". In many ways, the same applies to your homepage. People only need enough context to get started. Don't tell people you have lots of special offers. Show them the offers. Don't tell people you enable them to watch videos. Put your most popular video on the page and let them stop reading and start watching. The goal of your homepage is to get people to start interacting with your site, not to be an instruction manual for it.

Hot tip

People particularly like to see timely content on the homepage. Include links to your latest blog posts, press releases or products there. Update your homepage often, to show the site is lively.

Right: Google's first homepage from 1998, courtesy of The Wayback Machine (**web.archive. org**). Google has always let its search results speak for the company. The 1998 homepage enables you to search the web, with links for more information if you need it. Google is famous enough now to have dropped the "search the web" instructions. But they have always led by showing, not telling.

You are here...

One of the goals of your navigation is to show people where they are in the site. That provides context to help them understand the content, and also helps them to build a mental map of how big your site is and which sections they have already explored.

Giving each page a title

Every page of the site should have a unique title that appears immediately above its content. On a news article, the title might be the story headline. Reassure visitors by making your page title similar to the text on any links they followed to that page.

Using breadcrumb trails

Breadcrumb trails reveal the primary path through the website, by showing how the current page relates to other pages above it in the hierarchy. They don't necessarily show how somebody got to the page they are on: they just show the main route there. The different levels of the hierarchy are typically separated with greater-than signs, and each level is clickable so that people can easily jump up one or two levels. The last item in the trail is the current page, which shouldn't be a link because you're already there. For example, a breadcrumb trail might look like this:

Home > Books > Computing > Web Design in easy steps

Changing the navbar

Show people which section of the site they are in by changing its appearance on the navbar. Remember that people might not have clicked a link on the navbar to get there. They might have used a link in the middle of your page content, or a link on another site altogether. Cartoonist Scott McCloud (**www.scottmccloud.com**) uses lines from the icon to show the current section:

For your text links, you can have the color of visited links automatically changed by the browser so that people can understand where they have already been (see Chapter 7).

Don't remove the current page from the navbar. You might think it's illogical to offer a link to where the visitor already is, but people get more confused if the navbar changes shape or links move around in it, which is what happens when you remove links. As far as possible, your navbar should be standardized so that people can easily learn how to use it.

Adding a search engine

A search engine is an essential navigation feature for any but the smallest website. People don't want to trawl through links hunting for something specific: they want to just ask the computer to find it for them. You can add a Google search engine to any website.

1 Go to **https://programmablesearchengine.google.com/about/** and click the button to get started. You will need to log in with your Google account, or create a new one if you don't already have one.

2 Click **Add** to add a new search engine.

3 Give your search engine a name. If you set up multiple search engines, it helps you tell them apart.

Hot tip

The Google search engine can only provide results from Google's index of your site. That means it might lag behind your site updates and not be able to deliver the latest new pages. If you are using a blog system or content management system (CMS) (see Chapter 11), its search engine will be aware of all the latest content you've published using it.

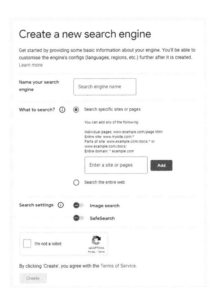

Create a new search engine

Get started by providing some basic information about your engine. You'll be able to customise the engine's configs (languages, regions, etc.) further after it is created. Learn more

Name your search engine   Search engine name

What to search? ⓘ ◉ Search specific sites or pages

You can add any of the following:

Individual pages: www.example.com/page.html
Entire site: www.mysite.com/*
Parts of site: www.example.com/docs/* or www.example.com/docs/
Entire domain: *.example.com

Enter a site or pages   **Add**

○ Search the entire web

Search settings ⓘ   ⬤ Image search
⬤ SafeSearch

☐ I'm not a robot   reCAPTCHA

By clicking 'Create', you agree with the Terms of Service.

Create

4 Into the box of sites to search, put your domain name, such as **www.example.com**, followed by /*. This will search the whole site. If you only want to include specific pages, you can list their full URLs here (for example, **www.example.com/books.html**) instead.

5 If you have more than one website, you can add them all so that your search engine returns results from them all.

Hot tip

If you subscribe to the Programmable Search Element Paid API, you can remove ads from your search results. Currently, it costs $5 per 1,000 searches. It might be a good investment to stop visitors leaking to your competitors' sites through ads on your site.

6 Enable **Image search** and/or **SafeSearch** if you want to use them. **SafeSearch** suppresses adult content.

7 Complete the box to confirm you're not a robot and click the **Create** button at the bottom of the page. You'll see confirmation your search engine has been created:

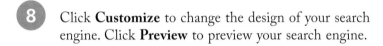

Your new search engine has been created

Copy the following code and paste it into your site's <body> section, where you want the search box and the search results to render.

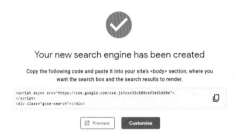

```
<script async src="https://cse.google.com/cse.js?cx=32c809ce33e31498e">
</script>
<div class="gcse-search"></div>
```

[Preview] [Customise]

8 Click **Customize** to change the design of your search engine. Click **Preview** to preview your search engine.

9 When you're ready, copy the search engine code. Paste it into your web page HTML, where you would like your search engine to appear.

10 Open the web page in your browser and test the search engine by typing in some keywords that should deliver pages from different parts of your website. The results appear in an overlay on top of your web page by default.

The look and feel settings enable you to show search results on a different web page from the one that hosts the search box, and to modify the search engine color scheme.

If you're a member of Google AdSense (www. google.com/adsense), Google will pay you when your site visitors click on the adverts in your search results.

Effective error messages

Beware

This will only work if you are using an Apache server and you have permission from your hosting company to change the .htaccess file. Seek technical support if you can't make it work: this is a tricky feature.

72

Sometimes things don't work out as they should, and you have to break the bad news to the visitor. Be gentle. In particular, avoid using language that accuses them of making a mistake or makes them feel like they've broken the site, when it almost certainly isn't their fault. It's better to offer practical advice on what they need to do next.

A common problem arises when you move or remove a web page, resulting in what's known as a 404 error when somebody tries to visit it. You can customize the 404 error page so that it helps to bring people back in to your site rather than representing a dead end, which encourages them to leave. Follow these steps:

1. Create your error page. Use your normal site template to reassure people they are still in your site, and provide links to your homepage and most popular pages. Your links need to have the full URL, such as **http://www.example. com/news.html**, instead of just news.html. Include a search box. Save the page as **404message.html**.

2. Create a text file called **htaccess.txt**. This file only needs to contain one line:
   ErrorDocument 404 /404message.html

3. Upload your htaccess.txt and 404message.html files to the top level of your server using FTP (see Chapter 12). Rename htaccess.txt on the server to .htaccess (a dot then "htaccess", with nothing before the dot).

4. Test it by trying to visit a page you know doesn't exist. If all's gone well, you will see your customized error page!

Right: An error page on the BBC website, with advice to check the website address was typed correctly, search the site or visit the homepage.

14 tips for effective links

Here are some principles that will help ensure your links are easy for everybody to use, whichever device or browser they prefer:

1 Be consistent. Don't use different names to refer to the same section of your website. Even using easily interchanged terms, like "store" and "shop", to refer to the same section can create the impression that you couldn't make up your mind about what to call it.

2 Avoid quirky names for sections on your site. People won't waste time clicking to see where they go. Use simple terms like "Forum", "Shop" and "Reviews".

3 Keep the text in your links short. The links should be signposts to other pages, not lengthy descriptions of them.

4 Make sure your links make sense in isolation. They draw the eye on screen, and screen readers can read all the links on a page to help visitors understand what they can do. Links that say "Click here" or "More..." help nobody.

5 Don't have links sharing the same text, unless they go to the same page.

6 Make sure your link text is descriptive enough so that people can understand what they might find behind it before they click. People will get frustrated if they click a link to find that they're not interested in what's behind it.

7 Don't tell people to click somewhere else. Don't say "click the Reviews button to find out more". Instead, provide a direct additional link to the Reviews section in the text.

8 Don't draw attention to the interface. Instead of saying "Click here to order the book", edit your link text so that it is a strong call to action – for example: "Order the book". People already know they have to click (or tap) that link to do so.

Hot tip

Search engines use your link text to understand what the linked page is about. Using clear, descriptive text helps with your search engine indexing.

Beware

Strike a balance between the number of clicks required to get somewhere, and making it obvious what the next click should be for any given visitor. You could link to every page from your homepage so that everywhere is just one click away. But nobody wants to try to make sense of 150 links. At the other extreme, if you only give people one option from a page, they'll get frustrated at the lack of control over their visit.

...cont'd

74

Beware

What's the most important navigation tool on any website? The browser's **Back** button. So, avoid any tricks that stop it from working, such as immediately diverting people to a different web page using JavaScript.

Hot tip

Test your links regularly. Broken links frustrate visitors and are seen as a sign of poor quality by search engines. There's a free link checker at **http://validator.w3.org/ checklink**

9 Make sure people can see what is a link at a glance. Don't make them work it out. By default, text links are blue and underlined. If that's consistent with your color scheme, using that link style will enable people to immediately recognize what is a link. If not, ensure that your links always contrast with the rest of your text, and always reserve the use of underlining for links, to avoid confusion.

10 Use plain HTML links (see Chapter 6) wherever possible. Humans and search engines alike might struggle to use JavaScript-based links.

11 If you link to something that isn't a standard web page, such as a PDF file, warn people by putting the name of the format in brackets toward the end of the link text. For example, you might have the link text "Download our new brochure (PDF)". This can be important for assistive devices that can't read non-HTML files.

12 If you're linking to an email address so that people can contact you, make sure it's obvious that the link goes to an email address. It can be disorientating if visitors expect a link to open a new web page and find it opens their email program instead.

13 Don't have links that only make sense when the mouse hovers over them, such as icons with explanatory text that only appears when the mouse rolls over them. It should be immediately obvious what a link does. Many devices (including touchscreen devices) can't simulate the mouse hovering, so their users can't make sense of those links.

14 One of our accessibility tips was not to open new windows without a warning. It's worth reiterating here because users are often confused by new windows. Sometimes they don't notice them, so they think the link hasn't worked. Other times, they get stuck in that window because they can't use the **Back** button to return.

6 HTML: The language of the web

Every web page is built using HTML, a special language for describing web content. In this chapter, you'll learn how it works, will be introduced to the most important tags, and will learn the principles of good HTML.

What is HTML?

HTML is the language of the internet. It's short for hypertext markup language, but don't let the jargon scare you off.

"Hypertext" is simply content that you navigate through using links, and "marking up" just means labeling the content so that the browser knows what to do with it.

A web page is basically a plain text file that can only contain keyboard characters. It can't have bold or italic formatting embedded in it, like a Word document can.

The browser ignores white space in an HTML file, too, so it doesn't even know where the paragraph breaks are. HTML includes instructions that explain to the browser how it should treat different parts of the page.

You create an HTML document by writing the text you want on your web page, and then adding *tags*. These are special pieces of code that use pointed brackets, which you might know better as greater-than/less-than signs. A < bracket is used to start a tag and a > bracket is used to end it. Tags often come in pairs so that they can mark the start and the end of text that should be treated in a particular way.

Here's some example HTML code:

```
<h1>This is the headline for the page</h1>
<p>Between the p tags, you find a paragraph.</p>
```

While the tags themselves might seem foreign, the idea is simple. The <h1> tag tells the browser that this is the most important headline on the page. The </h1> tag is used to mark the end of the headline.

The <p> and </p> tags are used to mark the start and end of the paragraph. When tags come in pairs, the second one uses a / to show it is a closing tag and not the start of the next tag.

You can create an HTML document using any text editor or word processor, such as Notepad or WordPad in Windows. Make sure you save as a text-only file, though, otherwise your file might include layout codes that the browser can't understand.

You can view the HTML for any web page on the internet. In your browser, right-click on the web page and select **View Source**.

Hot tip

HTML filenames usually end with .htm or .html. Use only lowercase characters and numbers in your filenames, and don't include any spaces. Instead, use a hyphen to separate words. The homepage on a website is usually index.htm or index.html.

Hot tip

To test an HTML file on your computer, open it in your web browser. In Chrome, use **Ctrl + O**.

Hot tip

It's not essential to use a </p> tag if a new <p> or <h1> tag implies that the previous paragraph ended. It's a good idea to use the tag, though, to avoid bugs later.

Structuring HTML pages

Although the content of web pages can be wildly different, the basic document structure is the same.

You can see the code for a simple web page I've made here:

```
<!DOCTYPE html>
<html lang="en">

<head>
      <title>Web Design in easy steps</title>
      <meta name="viewport" content="width=device-
            width, initial-scale=1.0">
</head>

<body>
      <h1>This is the headline for the page</h1>
      <p>Between the p tags, you find a paragraph.</p>
</body>

</html>
```

You don't need fancy tools to create HTML. I've used Notepad here. It's a free part of Windows.

An HTML document is divided into two parts:

- The head contains information about the document that doesn't appear as web page content. This is known as metadata. It includes search engine information (see Chapter 13) and links to style sheets for design (see Chapter 7). The head of the document starts with a <head> tag and ends with a </head> tag.

- The body contains the HTML code for your page content. This section includes the text, pictures and anything else you want users to experience. The body of the document starts with a <body> tag and ends with a </body> tag.

I've used indentation here so that you can see the document structure more clearly. It's optional in HTML.

This is what that file looks like in a browser window (I've resized the window to fit the content here so that you can see it better):

Tags are not case-sensitive. That means you can use H1 instead of h1 and doctype instead of DOCTYPE. It's common to use lowercase for all tags. DOCTYPE is the exception. It's usually styled in uppercase.

...cont'd

There are some more tags that HTML requires:

- The DOCTYPE tag is always the first line in your HTML document. It tells the browser which version of HTML the web page is using, and it's short for document type. My doctype is for HTML5, the latest version of HTML.

- The <html> and </html> tags mark the start and the end of the HTML document. Apart from the DOCTYPE tag, they're the first and last tags in the document. It's recommended to specify the language of the document in the opening <html> tag. I've used English (en).

These are the other tags in our example first page:

- The <title> and </title> tags go in the head and are used for the page title. This is the name of the browser window when someone is viewing your page, the name of the bookmark if you add the page to your browser favorites, and is used in search engine results when Google suggests your web page. Ensure each page you create has a unique title.

- The <meta> tag in the head of the document is being used here to set the viewport size. The viewport is the visible area of the web page. Without it, some mobile devices might try to show a desktop-sized viewport, zoomed out. This tag makes your web page much easier to use on mobile devices, and is a first step toward creating a responsive design.

Hot tip

You've already met the <h1> tag, but note that the on-screen headline doesn't have to be the same as the content of the <title> tag.

Right: The web page is shown without the meta tag to set the viewport. The iPhone here shows the web page as it would appear on a desktop device. Users can zoom in, but it's not an easy user experience.

Far right: With the addition of the meta tag to set the viewport, the text is much easier to read.

Adding pictures

To add a picture to your web page, use the <img> tag. You need to include four pieces of information, known as attributes:

- The *image source.* If your image file is in the same folder as the HTML file, then the image source will simply be its filename. Otherwise, you'll need to say which folder it's in, too. You can include images on different websites by adding the domain name and full path to the file, but you should get permission from that website first.

- The *width* and the *height* of the image in pixels. Including this helps the browser to speed up its display of the web page, because it knows how much space to set aside for pictures. If your image looks distorted, check the width and height attributes in your <img> tag. The browser displays your image at the size you specify, even if the image is a different size.

- *Alternative text* for people who can't see the image. They might be people using a screen reader or someone who has switched images off because they have a poor connection. The alternative text should not contain additional or different information to the image. (You'll hear people call it an alt tag, but it's not, strictly speaking, a tag. It's the alt attribute.)

Here is an example <img> tag:

```
<img src="dog.jpg" width="250" height="150" alt="My
dog gnawing a bone" loading="lazy">
```

This adds an image called dog.jpg into the web page with a width of 250 pixels and a height of 150 pixels. If the picture was in a folder called photos on a website called **www.example.com**, you would change the src attribute to "**http://www.example.com/ photos/dog.jpg**".

The final part of the tag enables lazy loading. Normally, when you visit a web page, the browser downloads all of its images straight away. This is called eager loading.

With lazy loading, the browser doesn't download an image unless you're actually going to see it. The images near the top are downloaded and shown as normal, but images further down the page aren't downloaded until they're about to be scrolled into view. Using lazy loading helps to speed up web pages, and avoids downloading images unnecessarily.

CSS code can override the width and height values in the <img> tag.

The <img> tag (like some others) doesn't have a closing tag. Some people put a / before the tag's > bracket. It's not required, but it's not forbidden either and you might see it in other web pages.

Take care with the size of your images. Before putting them on your website, resize and compress them.

...cont'd

In a responsive website, you might want to serve different images depending on the size of the viewport. The <picture> tag enables you to do this. You use it together with an <img> tag, like this:

```
<picture>
        <source media="(min-width: 900px)"
                srcset="pies-big.jpg">
        <img src="pies-small.jpg"
                alt="Home made mince pies">
</picture>
```

In this example, the browser uses the pies_big.jpg image file if the viewport is more than 900 pixels wide (900px). Otherwise, it uses the pies_small.jpg file. You can add more <source> tags for other images to serve at other sizes. The final <img> tag contains the default image. You can speed up your website by ensuring that images are sized appropriately. Small-screen devices do not need to download unnecessarily big image files, for example.

The <picture> tag also gives you creative options. While images can be resized easily in the browser using CSS, not all images work well at all sizes. In the example below, I show a different close-up image on smaller viewports rather than simply scale down the large image:

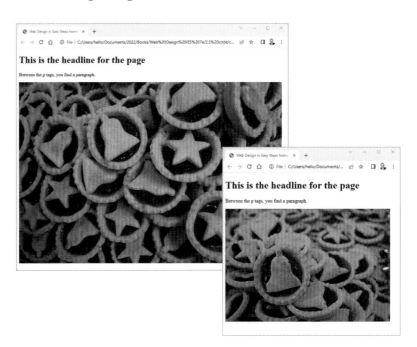

Hot tip

The quote marks around attributes are optional, but many designers prefer to use them.

Hot tip

The <picture> tag can also be used to offer browsers different image formats so that they can pick the most efficient one they support.

Hot tip

You can also use the srcset attribute in the <img> tag to provide a number of different image sizes for the browser to choose from. It's time-consuming creating the separate image files, but a content management system (CMS) such as WordPress can do it for you automatically in the background.

Adding audio and video

There are two tags that can be used to embed audio and video into your web page. The audio player (shown on the right) can include playback controls and has a menu to change the playback speed and download the file. Here's some code to add an audio file:

```
<audio src="filename.mp3" controls loop preload="none">
<p>Your browser cannot play this audio content.</p>
<p><a href="filename.mp3">Download the MP3</a>.</p>
</audio>
```

There is a similar video tag:

```
<video src="filename.mp4" controls autoplay muted>
<p>Your browser does not support this video.</p>
</video>
```

The HTML content between the <audio> and </audio> tags, and between the <video> and </video> tags, is only shown in browsers that do not support those tags. The opening tag contains all the settings and information for the media player:

- The **src** attribute points to the name of the file. MP3 files are most widely supported in audio and MP4 in video.

- The **controls** attribute tells the browser to include playback controls. Without it, videos can play without any controls.

- The **loop** attribute tells the browser to endlessly repeat the audio or video. You can remove this attribute.

- The **preload** attribute can be set to "none", "auto" or "metadata". It gives the browser a hint about the available server bandwidth. Using "none" avoids the content being preloaded, reducing the burden on the server. Using "metadata" hints to the browser that it can download information about the file but that server bandwidth is limited. Using "auto" tells the browser it can download the media straight away without worrying about the server.

- The **autoplay** attribute sets the media to play when the page loads.

- The **muted** attribute sets a video to play silently, but users can use the controls to turn the volume up.

You can add a width attribute to the video tag to control how big the video is on screen.

You can upload your video to YouTube and share it from there (see Chapter 3). Soundcloud (www.soundcloud.com) and Bandcamp (www.bandcamp.com) offer a similar service for podcasts and music.

Browsers try to protect their users from unwanted audio, so autoplay with sound doesn't always work. It depends on how the user has interacted with the site previously.

When linking to other people's websites, the page reference you use as the href attribute in your anchor tag is the same as what you see in the address bar of your browser, when you visit the web page.

Adding links

What makes the web so effective is the ability to link to any other website or web page, anywhere on the web. To add a link in HTML, use an anchor tag, like this:

```
<a href="booking.html">Book your ticket!</a>
```

The href attribute tells the browser where the link goes, and the text between the anchor tags is the link text displayed on screen.

When a website visitor clicks on that text, they are taken to the booking.html page, which is in the same folder as the page they are currently reading.

Linking to files in different folders

If it was in a subfolder called shop, you'd use:

```
<a href="shop/booking.html">Book your ticket!</a>
```

Perhaps you want to link to a file in the folder above the one that contains the HTML file with the link? In that case, you'd use ../ at the start, like this:

```
<a href="../booking.html">Book your ticket!</a>
```

You can move around the directory tree by combining these ideas. For example, you can go up a level and then go down into a different subfolder, like this:

```
<a href="../news/index.html">Our latest news</a>
```

You don't have to link to HTML files. You could link to an image file or a PDF that visitors can download by following your link.

Adding external links

You can also link to another website, or a specific page on it. To link to Google, for example, you would use:

```
<a href="https://www.google.com">Visit Google</a>
```

You can use an image as a link instead of text, by replacing the link display text with an image tag, like this:

```
<a href="booking.html"><img src="bookingadvert.gif" width="150" height="50" alt="Book now!"></a>
```

Image links like this are used on lots of websites to make product pictures link to further information about the products.

If you're linking to another website, don't forget the "https://" in the link destination. If you just link to "**www.google.com**", it won't work.

Adding email links

You can also link to an email address. When the link is clicked, it will open a new email in the default email program. Here's some example code:

```
<a href="mailto:webmaster@example.com">Email me</a>
```

Make it obvious that the link is to an email address and not another web page.

Linking within a document

You can add a link to a specific part of a web page. Here's how:

1 Make up a unique ID name for the location you'd like to link to in your document. Then, add the ID attribute to the appropriate tag in your web content. You can link to a <div> tag (see page 95), but equally can use a <p> or <h1> tag or any other tag. Here, I'm using the <h1> heading:
```
<h1 id="news">Latest news headlines</h1>
```

2 Create an <a> tag and use a # symbol together with the ID you'd like to link to:
```
<a href="#news">Jump to news headlines</a>
```

3 When you click that link, you'll see your browser jumps straight to that part of the page, without reloading it.

4 If you want to link to a page fragment like this from another web page, use the web page's filename or URL and add the # symbol and ID on the end, like this:
```
<a href="index.html#news">See our news</a>
```

Hot tip

Sometimes it can be helpful to open a new window – for example, to show terms and conditions. You can use the target attribute on a link to suggest a new window:

```
<a href="terms.html"
target="_blank">
See terms and conditions
</a>
```

83

Left: Wikipedia uses many types of links. The picture links to a larger version. The **Contents** box on an article provides links to jump to the sections down the page. The left navigation and summary box on the right provide links to other pages on the site.

Creating tables

HTML includes tags to enable you to lay out tabular information, such as a timetable or anything else that you might easily describe in a spreadsheet. The following picture shows Wikipedia using a table to communicate the capital city, size and population for Germany's 16 states:

You could put an image tag inside a table cell, so you could include the state flag, for example. You can add links for more information, too, or any other HTML code.

Constituent states

Main article: States of Germany

Germany comprises sixteen states which are collectively referred to as *Länder*.[76] Each state has its own state constitution[77] and is largely autonomous in regard to its internal organisation. Because of differences in size and population the subdivisions of these states vary, especially as between city states (*Stadtstaaten*) and states with larger territories (*Flächenländer*). For regional administrative purposes five states, namely Baden-Württemberg, Bavaria, Hesse, North Rhine-Westphalia and Saxony, consist of a total of 22 Government Districts (*Regierungsbezirke*). As of 2009 Germany is divided into 403 districts (*Kreise*) at a municipal level; these consist of 301 rural districts and 102 urban districts.[78]

State	Capital	Area (km²)	Population
Baden-Württemberg	Stuttgart	35,752	10,753,880
Bavaria	Munich	70,549	12,538,696
Berlin	Berlin	892	3,460,725
Brandenburg	Potsdam	29,477	2,503,273
Bremen	Bremen	404	660,999
Hamburg	Hamburg	755	1,786,448
Hesse	Wiesbaden	21,115	6,067,021
Mecklenburg-Vorpommern	Schwerin	23,174	1,642,327
Lower Saxony	Hanover	47,618	7,918,293
North Rhine-Westphalia	Düsseldorf	34,043	17,845,154
Rhineland-Palatinate	Mainz	19,847	4,003,745
Saarland	Saarbrücken	2,569	1,017,567
Saxony	Dresden	18,416	4,149,477
Saxony-Anhalt	Magdeburg	20,445	2,335,006
Schleswig-Holstein	Kiel	15,763	2,834,259
Thuringia	Erfurt	16,172	2,235,025

Marking up a table

The HTML code for tables can look complex because you have to indicate the start and end of the table, each row and each cell, resulting in a lot of HTML in a small space. But the tags are fairly intuitive:

Remember to include closing tags. Old browsers can struggle to display the page if you forget to close your <table> tag with a </table> tag.

- <table> and </table> mark the start and end of the table.

- <caption> and </caption> encapsulate a title for the table that summarizes its content.

- <tr> and </tr> go around each table row.

- <th> and <th> go around each table heading cell. You can have a heading on a column or at the start of a row.

- <td> and </td> go around each table data item (which means each box of information on the table).

...cont'd

You can see the markup for a simple table of population values below. I've kept the table to three rows and four columns to avoid overcomplicating it. The first row is made up of headings for the columns. The next row starts with a heading to say which state that row refers to, and then includes the different data items:

Hot tip

The top-left cell of a table could be a heading for its row or column. That's why its <th> tag includes a scope attribute, to explain that it's describing the content below it. This doesn't change what's on screen, but it helps with accessibility.

```
tables-example.htm - Notepad

File  Edit  Format  View  Help
<table>

<caption>Population of the United
States by State</caption>

<tr>
<th scope="col">State</th>
<th>Population</th>
<th>Density</th>
<th>Ranking by population</th>
</tr>

<tr>
<th>California</th>
<td>36.9 million</td>
<td>90.49/km2</td>
<td>1st</td>
</tr>

<tr>
<th>Nevada</th>
<td>2.6 million</td>
<td>9.02/km2</td>
<td>7th</td>
</tr>

<tr>
<th>Minnesota</th>
<td>5.2 million</td>
<td>25.21/km2</td>
<td>21st</td>
</tr>

</table>
```

This is what that table looks like in a browser:

Population of the United States by State

State	Population	Density	Ranking by population
California	36.9 million	90.49/km2	1st
Nevada	2.6 million	9.02/km2	7th
Minnesota	5.2 million	25.21/km2	21st

The headings, such as "Population" and "Density", are wrapped in <th> tags and appear bold on screen by default. I've added a border to the table for clarity here. You'll learn how to improve the presentation of your HTML in the next chapter.

Hot tip

So that blind visitors don't have to remember too much, the screen reader can read the appropriate table heading before a data item. That's why I've made the state name a heading for each row: as well as being a data item, it provides useful context for the rest of the row.

...cont'd

Column1	Column2	Column3	Column4
Cell data	Cell data	Cell data	Cell data
rowspan="2"	Cell data	Cell data	Cell data
	Cell data	colspan="2"	
Cell data	Cell data	Cell data	Cell data

An example table, showing the effect of using rowspan and colspan.

Hot tip

In the early days of the web, tables were used to lay out entire web pages. There are much better options now, as you'll see in Chapter 8.

Hot tip

Keep an eye on how big your table is. There's no technical limitation, but big tables are hard to use. If people have to trace their finger across the screen or scroll it to read your table, it may be too big.

Creating cells that span multiple cells

Sometimes, you might want table cells to be different sizes. You might want one cell to have the same height as two cells to the right of it, or you might want one cell to stretch across two columns underneath it, for example. You can modify the <td> (or <th>) tag with a rowspan or colspan attribute to achieve this:

```
<td rowspan="2">This cell is two cells deep</td>
```

When you use this markup, the cell stretches to occupy the space of the cell underneath it, too, so you will need one fewer cell on the next row. If you set the column span to 2, it will stretch to occupy the cell to its right as well, so you will need one fewer cell in the same row. You can have a colspan or rowspan attribute of any value, so you can represent complex data.

Using <thead>, <tfoot> and <tbody> tags

You can mark up the head, body and foot of your table. When long tables are printed and span multiple pages, the browser can print the table head and foot at the top and bottom of the table data on each page. Here's some template code for a table containing two rows of data and a head and foot:

```
<table>
<thead>
      <tr>
            <th>Column heading</th>
            <th>Column heading</th>
            <th>Column heading</th>
</thead>
<tbody>
      <tr>
            <td>Data item</td>
            <td>Data item</td>
            <td>Data item</td>
      <tr>
            <td>Data item</td>
            <td>Data item</td>
            <td>Data item</td>
</tbody>
<tfoot>
      <tr>
            <td>Column footer</td>
            <td>Column footer</td>
            <td>Column footer</td>
</tfoot>
</table>
```

Creating lists

Sometimes all you need are simple bullet points to get your message across.

HTML includes tags for marking up bulleted lists (known as unordered lists) and numbered lists (known as ordered lists). You can change the format of the numbers or bullets using CSS.

You can also use a list to mark up the links in a navbar, and then use CSS to change the default layout so that the items are displayed side by side on screen, but can be easily navigated as a list when using devices like screen readers.

To create a list, start with a <ul> or <ol> tag for an unordered or ordered list. Then, put an <li> tag before each list item. You can optionally use a closing tag of </li> at the end of each item, if you want to.

Here's some HTML content that includes a numbered list:

```
<p>There are 5 Die Hard films:</p>
<ol>
<li>Die Hard
<li>Die Hard 2: Die Harder
<li>Die Hard With a Vengeance
<li>Live Free or Die Hard
<li>A Good Day to Die Hard
</ol>
<p>These all star Bruce Willis.</p>
```

The screenshot below shows what it looks like on screen. Note that, by default, each list item starts on a new line, and that the text after the list starts a new block of text on screen, even without a new paragraph tag:

Beware

If you forget your closing </ol> or </ul> tag, the rest of your web page's paragraphs might be indented on screen.

There are 5 Die Hard films:

1. Die Hard
2. Die Hard 2: Die Harder
3. Die Hard With a Vengeance
4. Live Free or Die Hard
5. A Good Day to Die Hard

These all star Bruce Willis.

What is a web form?

One basic way that visitors can interact with a website is by using a web form. The form analogy comes from paper forms, such as a job application form. A web form provides boxes where people can enter their information or select from options.

Below, you can see the form that Facebook uses to gather your details when you register for a Facebook account:

You can find PHP scripts online that can receive the data that visitors enter into your form and email it to you.

You can also find scripts online that are hosted on other people's servers. These will send your visitors' data to them first, and they will then make it available to you. If you use one of these scripts, make sure the provider is reputable.

You could use a form on your website for any of the following:

- **A contact form.** Not as friendly for visitors as publishing an email address, but it means you can hide your email address from spammers. You can also prompt visitors with questions and give a box for each answer to encourage a response.

- **A search engine.** Make it easy for people to find what they need, by enabling them to type in some descriptive keywords so that you can find them all the pages that match.

- **An order form.** The easier it is for someone to buy from you, the more likely they are to do it. Enable them to enter their order requirements on your website, including delivery details and payment information.

HTML is used to structure the form, but you'll need a different technology to handle what the visitor enters into it. You might have a script (or program) on the server, for example, that returns search results or forwards their message to you by email, or you might use JavaScript to update the screen in response to the input.

Choosing form elements

There are several standard elements you can choose from to design a form in HTML. You've almost certainly used them all before when visiting other websites. They are:

- **A textbox.** This is used to accept a single line of text input, such as a name or an email address. It is possible to type more into a textbox than can be seen on screen at once, because the box scrolls. To make it easy to use, give it enough screen space so that people can see everything they are typing.

- **A textarea.** This is like a textbox, except that it enables people to enter multiple lines of information. You might use it to accept comments on a contact form. You could use a textarea to accept an address, but that information will be more useful and complete if you prompt people to enter each line (street address, town, state, etc.) into a different textbox. Only use a textarea where the format of the data doesn't really matter.

- **Radio buttons.** These are used to choose only one option from a group. If one button is selected, all the others are automatically de-selected. They might be used to ask for information, such as age group, where the answers are mutually exclusive. Radio buttons are round.

- **Checkboxes.** These enable people to choose options by checking a box beside them. People can check multiple boxes, so they might be used to indicate a number of different interests. Checkboxes are square.

- **Select menus.** These save screen space by only opening up their options when clicked. They are harder to use than radio buttons or checkboxes, and should only be used for options that can be easily navigated when users can't see all the options at once. They're most often used to complete an address using an alphabetically sorted list of countries.

- **Buttons.** Every form needs a button that people can click to confirm they've finished completing it. It's often called a **Submit** button, but it might actually say something else on it. For example, Google's button says "Google Search" and eBay's button for logging in says "Sign in". Pressing the **Enter** key should have the same effect as clicking the **Submit** button.

Textbox

Name:
Sean McManus

Textarea

Your feedback:
I thought it was great, but I'd like to learn more about the origin story of the characters.

Radio button

Are you..?
○ Under 18
◉ 18 or older

Checkbox

Do you like listening to..?
☑ Pop
☑ Rock
☐ Classical
☐ Jazz

Select

State: Choose one... ▾
Choose one...
Alabama
Sub Alaska
Arizona
Submit form!

Above: Form elements, as seen in the Chrome browser.

You can change the size of a textbox on screen to 20 characters by adding size="20" to its tag. This only affects how much you can see at once, not how much can be entered into the box. To limit the text that can be entered to 20 characters, use maxlength="20".

Hot tip

The <br> tag adds a line break.

Hot tip

Labels make form elements easier to use for everyone. You can click a textbox's label to put your cursor in it, and can click a radio button's label to select it.

Using the <input> tag

Here is a simple newsletter subscription form that just asks visitors to enter their email address:

```
<form method="post" action="senddata.php">
<label for="email_address">Email address:</label>
<input type="text" id="email_address" name="email_
address" placeholder="yourname@example.com" required>
<input type="submit" value="Subscribe">
</form>
```

This is what it looks like on screen:

The <form> and </form> tags wrap the whole form. The action part of the tag tells the web browser where to send this data, in this code, to a script called senddata on the same server as the form itself. This form won't actually do anything when you submit it if you don't have a script to process the form data.

A textbox is just a hole on the screen, so you need to add some text near it to explain what should be entered into it. So that screen readers know which explanation belongs to which form element, you wrap <label> and </label> tags around it. You specify which form element the label belongs to by making the **for** attribute in the label the same as the **ID** attribute in the <input> tag. Designers typically position labels on screen above or to the left of the form element for text fields and to the right of radio buttons or checkboxes. I've also included a placeholder hint here, which appears inside the form box until the user starts typing into it.

The <input> tag has several attributes. The **type** attribute specifies the type of input, in this case an email address. The **ID** attribute is used to uniquely identify the element so that it can be associated with a label or so that CSS can be used to change its appearance later. To help you untangle the data when it comes through to your script, the **name** attribute is submitted along with the form data. To avoid confusion when you're building the site, the name can be the same as the ID attribute, as it is here, but it doesn't have to be.

If the **required** attribute is included in the <input> tag (as it is here), the browser won't allow the form to be submitted unless the textbox is completed.

The table below outlines the other input types you can use. To add a set of radio buttons for two age groups, for example, with the labels to the right of them, insert the following code. It can go anywhere between the <form> and </form> tags:

```
<input type="radio" value="under-18"
id="under-18" name="age">
<label for="under-18">Under 18</label>
<br>
<input type="radio" value="over-18"
id="over-18" name="age">
<label for="over-18">18 or older</label>
```

Some touchscreen devices show a different keyboard for email, number and URL input types. This helps users enter data quickly.

If you want to make a particular radio button or checkbox selected by default, put the word **checked** before the closing bracket of its <input> tag. The value attribute defines which data will be sent to the server when the form is submitted.

Form element	Input type	Notes
textbox	text	See example on facing page.
radio button	radio	All radio buttons with the same name attribute belong to the same group, only one of which can be selected.
checkbox	checkbox	Each checkbox should have a unique name attribute.
submit button	submit	The value attribute defines the text that will appear on the button.
reset button (clear form)	reset	The value attribute defines the text that will appear on the button.
password box	password	This functions the same as a textbox, except that what is typed in is not shown on screen. Dots are used to show the number of characters typed.
email address box	email	The browser does some basic checks on the data to check it looks like an email address.
website address box	url	The browser checks for a valid website address.
phone number box	tel	Mobile devices show a number keypad for quick entry.
date box	date	Devices can show a date picker. Add the attribute of value="2025-12-25" to set the starting date in YYYY-MM-DD format.
number box	number	`<input type="number" min="10" max="20">` will make the browser show a warning if the user enters values outside the minimum of 10 and maximum of 20.

Using other form elements

The <input> tag is used to create nearly all form elements, but there are two more form elements that use their own tags.

Creating a multiline textbox

A textbox with multiple lines is created using the <textarea> tag. The cols attribute gives the width on screen in characters, and the rows attribute is the height of the box in lines of text. Users can enter more information, and the box will scroll to accommodate it. Note that a closing </textarea> tag is required, even if there's nothing between the tags, as in this example:

```
<label for="comments">Your feedback:</label>
<textarea id="comments" name="comments" cols="20"
rows="5">
</textarea>
```

Creating select menus

To create a select menu, you use a combination of two new tags. The <select> and </select> tags go at the start and the end of the menu. Within them, you put your options, each one marked up with an <option> and </option> tag.

The value attribute on the <option> tag defines what will be submitted if that particular option is selected. It doesn't have to be the same as what is presented to the user. In my example below, the user might select "Alabama" on screen, but the server will be sent the code of "AL":

```
<label for="state">State:</label><select id="state"
name="state">
<option value="--" selected>Choose one...</option>
<option value="AL">Alabama</option>
<option value="AK">Alaska</option>
<option value="AZ">Arizona</option>
<!-- other state options go here -->
</select>
```

To set the default value for a select menu, add the word "selected" to its <option> tag, as I have here for the first option.

People who don't choose anything might have their preference indicated as the first item in your list when the form is submitted. By adding a "Choose one..." option and making it the default item, you can easily see when this has happened.

Adding autocomplete suggestions to a text field

You can add autocomplete suggestions to an input field so that the browser helps the user complete what they're typing when it recognizes it. In this screenshot, I've started to type "aus..." and the browser offers me "Austria" and "Australia" as options. I can select one of those options to save any more typing. I can also browse the menu of suggested options:

The feature that enables this is called a datalist. The <datalist> tag contains its name in the **ID** attribute, and surrounds a set of options. You add the list name in your <input> tag to associate it with the datalist. Try this:

```
<input type="text" name="country" placeholder="Your
country" list="countries">

<datalist id="countries">
      <option value="Austria"></option>
      <option value="Australia"></option>
      <option value="Canada"></option>
      <option value="France"></option>
      <option value="Germany"></option>
      <option value="UK"></option>
      <option value="USA">
            </option>
</datalist>
```

The functionality looks similar to an select menu, but there is one key difference. The user can select from the options available, like a select menu, but they can also override them. If they type something completely different into the textbox, the browser will allow it.

Hot tip

It takes time to enter information into a website, and users will be put off by a long and complicated form. Only ask for essential information. If you do need a long form, consider splitting the process over multiple short screens. This makes the process more approachable and also gives you a chance to follow up on incomplete submissions if you collect basic contact details first.

93

Beware

If you are going to ask people to enter personal and payment information into a form, make sure you have a secure server that encrypts the data as it crosses the internet. Your hosting company can help with this.

Adding iframes

Using the `<iframe>` tag, you can embed another web page or resource inside your web page. It's most useful for adding content to your web page from another website, such a YouTube video or Google Map. In Chapter 3, you saw how to get some HTML code from these sites using the `<iframe>` tag that you can paste into your site. Here's an example code snippet:

```
<iframe src="https://www.example.com/shared/page1.
html" name="my_iframe" width="600" height="450"
allowfullscreen loading="lazy"></iframe>
```

This is what the attributes mean:

- The **src** attribute points to the name of the file you want in the iframe. Often, this will be on another server.

- The **name** attribute gives this iframe a name. It enables you to load content into it from the web page by using a link with a target of the iframe name:

```
<a href="https://www.example.com/shared/page2.html"
target="my_iframe">See more offers</a>
```

- The **width** and **height** attributes set the size of the iframe.

- The **allowfullscreen** attribute allows the iframe to use the browser's full-screen viewing feature.

- The **loading** attribute enables you to set the iframe to load only when it will be seen by the user (lazy loading). This helps to speed up your user's experience on your website.

If your content is too big to fit the iframe, the browser will show scrollbars.

When you put someone else's content in an iframe on your site, you're using their content and their server bandwidth. It's considered polite to get permission first.

Right: Here, I've embedded a Wikipedia page inside my web page. The iframe isn't big enough for the content, so horizontal and vertical scrollbars have been added.

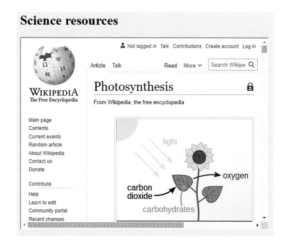

Dividing the page up

There are two reasons for dividing your page up logically:

- Using CSS (see Chapter 7), you can change the appearance and position of different sections of HTML content.

- Marking sections logically enables browsers and search engines to understand your page content better. For example, they can help readers find your navbar or content quickly.

The modern way to mark up your web page is to use a set of tags that were introduced with HTML5 for the different parts of the page. They are:

- <header>, which is used for introductory or navigational aids.

- <nav>, which is used for a significant group of navigation links.

- <main>, which is used to indicate the main page content.

- <section>, which is used to mark up thematically linked content. It can be used as a wrapper around related content so that a style (such as a border) can be applied to it.

- <article>, which is used for an article.

- <aside>, which is used for loosely related information, such as a pullquote or a sidebar.

- <footer>, which is used to provide more information, such as copyright information.

Each one is closed using a close tag, such as </nav> or </aside>.

You can also use <div> and </div> tags to indicate the start and end of a section in your code. Before the new HTML5 tags, that's what designers had to do for everything. It was messy having so many <div> tags, but you'll probably still want to use some today.

These new tags enable more meaningful HTML so that browsers and search engines can help users navigate your content easily. The tags give you a lot of flexibility in how you structure your web page. You can have an article inside a section or a section inside an article, for example. Each article could have its own header and footer, or you might just have one of each for the whole page.

If you just want to mark up a few words in the middle of a sentence, you put <span> and </span> tags around them. Think first, though, whether you would be better off using <em> or <strong> tags to indicate emphasis or something of greater importance. The <span> tag doesn't mean anything, but those other tags do.

You can put <div> sections inside each other. When you use a </div> tag, it always closes the most recent <div> tag that is still open.

...cont'd

Here's a web page as it might appear on a computer, together with the code to structure it. I used a div around the whole page so that I could style all the page content with CSS (see Chapter 7):

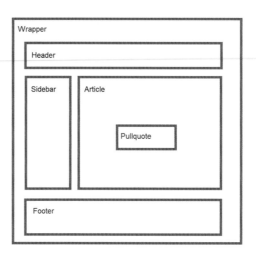

Hot tip

Your article can contain pictures, videos or any other content.

Beware

This HTML doesn't do anything to change the presentation of your article by itself. You'll need to use CSS to actually create the boxes.

```html
<div class="wrapper">
<header>
      <p>Site branding here</p>
      <nav>
            <a href="index.html">Home</a>
            <a href="news.html">News</a>
            <a href="blog.html">Blog</a>
            <a href="shop.html">Shop</a>
      </nav>
</header>

<main>
      <aside><p>Sidebar HTML here</p></aside>
      <article>
            <h1>Article heading here</h1>
            <p>Article starts here</p>
            <aside><p>Pullquote here</p></aside>
            <p>Article ends here.</p>
      </article>
</main>

<footer>
      <p>Footer information about my site</p>
      <p>It can include links to other pages</p>
</footer>
</div>
```

The art of good HTML

The purpose of HTML has changed over the years. In the early days of the commercial web, HTML was used to lay out a web page and format it visually. It included a mix of the content and the design. Now, as you will see in Chapter 7, we use CSS for formatting, and HTML should be used primarily for marking up the structure of your content.

That means your HTML should be adding meaning to your content, and should be reasonably independent of the on-screen appearance. If you're dictating the design of your web page in HTML, you're doing it wrong!

Choosing the right tags to mark up your content

You've already seen how the <h1> tag can be used to indicate the most important headline on a page. There are also tags for <h2>, <h3>, all the way down to <h6>. In practice, people rarely use headings deeper than <h3>.

The headings will (by default) be different sizes on screen, with the <h1> heading being the largest. You can't just use <h1> to make text big and <h6> to make it small, though: you have to use the heading tags for headlines, otherwise your HTML doesn't make sense. Remember that your HTML won't always be used on a computer screen: sometimes screen readers will use your markup to navigate between sections of the page, and sometimes search engines will use it to work out what's important when indexing your site.

Similarly, the <strong> tag will usually make text bold. Its proper use, though, is not to change what the text looks like, but to indicate text that has strong importance. The <em> tag for emphasis typically shows italicized text, but should be used only for text that you would emphasize when reading it out. If you use tags like these to mark up large areas of text, just to change their appearance in your browser, you make the web page potentially meaningless – or at least hard to use – for other devices.

Ask yourself whether the markup you're adding helps people to navigate your content using any device, or whether it is specific to what the web page looks like on your computer screen.

If it's specific to a computer screen, consider whether you can use CSS to achieve the same effect instead.

To make your document logical, you have to use the heading tags in order so that a <h3> heading can only appear inside a section titled with a <h2> heading, which is, itself, inside a section titled with a <h1> heading.

This is heading 1

This is heading 2

This is heading 3

This is heading 4

This is heading 5

This is heading 6

Headings 1 to 6, as seen in Google Chrome.

...cont'd

Keeping accessibility in mind

It's easy to do the wrong thing with HTML. You could fake table headings using fancy formatting, or omit labels from your forms. If you feed sloppy HTML into a browser, it won't warn you. It'll just do its best with whatever you throw at it. But if you don't mark up tables or forms correctly, they may become unusable by those who depend on assistive devices. The more accessible your HTML is, the more likely it is to work on devices you haven't tested and on new devices that are released.

Commenting your code

The examples in this chapter are simple, but a real web page can be extremely complicated. When you come back to modify a page later, it can be hard to understand the markup. To avoid confusion, add comments to your HTML by putting `<!--` at the start and `-->` at the end of the comment, like this:

```
</div> <!-- Closes wrapper div -->
```

These comments are not presented to the site visitor but can be seen if anybody views your source. Add comments to help you remember why you coded something the way you did.

The finished HTML

Your finished HTML web page will look pretty unremarkable, as you can see in my example below. All the content will be in a single column that fills the page width, and all the text will be black. But the content should look like it's structured logically. In the next chapter, you will learn how to change the layout and appearance of your web page:

Don't forget

Even when your website is in its early stages, you can ask people to test it and give you feedback. It's best to test your website early and often so that you can refine the design throughout, and don't incur a lot of rework at the end.

Validating your HTML

It's a good idea to make sure your page meets the HTML standard, even if it looks okay in your browser.

1 In your browser, visit **http://validator.w3.org**. It is the validator created by the World Wide Web Consortium (W3C for short). W3C develops the HTML standards.

2 Use the tabs to choose how you'd like to give the validator your code. You can validate an online page (**Validate by URI**), validate by uploading your HTML file, or validate by pasting code (**Validate by Direct Input**).

3 The results are graded. Errors are the most severe and should be fixed. Warnings offer you advice for things you should look into. **Info** results are the lowest priority.

4 Click the **Message Filtering** button at the top of your results for a summary of the issues.

Don't forget

The HTML standard helps to ensure that people can use your web page, no matter which device they use.

Hot tip

The messages include links to more information about the issue, and how it can be fixed.

Hot tip

Some of the issues flagged can be complex. While you're learning, don't worry too much about anything you don't understand. Prioritize the errors and warnings so that you can fix the biggest issues.

Reference: structure

Hot tip

You can add a comment to your HTML to help you remember how your web page works. The browser ignores comments. By surrounding a chunk of HTML with comment symbols, you can hide it from the browser and switch it off. This is what a comment looks like:

`<!-- comment -->`

HTML tag	Description
`<!DOCTYPE html>`	Defines the version of HTML being used. This simple doctype is for HTML5.
`<html>...<html>`	Used to indicate the start and end of the HTML document.
`<head>...</head>`	Used to define the boundaries of the head of the document, where meta tags and CSS links go.
`<title>...</title>`	Used to mark the title of the web page, which will be its link text in search engine listings and its default bookmark title. The title goes inside the <head> tags.
`<body>...</body>`	Used to define the boundaries of the body of the document, where the marked-up content is.
`<div>...</div>`	Used to mark the start and end of a section of content. A <div> section can enclose large chunks of content for styling.
`<span>...</span>`	Marks the start and end of a piece of content within a paragraph or heading.
`<header>...</header>`	Used for introductory or navigational aids.
`<footer>...</footer>`	Used for additional information, such as copyright details.
`<nav>...</nav>`	Used for a significant group of navigation links or a navbar.
`<article>...</article>`	The start and end of an article.
`<section>...</section>`	Indicates the start and end of a logical content section.
`<aside>...</aside>`	Indicates loosely related content, such as a pullquote or sidebar.
`<main>...</main>`	Marks the main page content.

Reference: head

Meta tags and title tag
These tags help search engines find your page (see Chapter 13) and make sure it looks good on mobile phones.

```
<title>Page title goes here</title>
<meta name="description" content="Description goes
here">
<meta name="viewport" content="width=device-
      width, initial-scale=1.0">
```

The meta tags, style sheet link, and favorites icons links go between your <head> and </head> tags.

Adding a style sheet
See Chapter 7 for an explanation of style sheets. To add an external style sheet, use this line:

```
<link href="folder/filename.css" rel="stylesheet">
```

Adding an external JavaScript file
JavaScript (see Chapter 9) sometimes needs to be added between the <head> and </head> tags, but it can go anywhere in your web page (depending on the script). The page will often load faster if the script is put just before the </body> tag. To add a JavaScript file to your web page, use this line:

```
<script src="folder/filename.js"></script>
```

Adding favorites icons
You can add an icon to your web page, called a favicon, which appears in bookmarks and on browser tabs. It should be a 32 x 32 pixel .ico format image file. You can make one using the free program IrfanView (**www.irfanview.com**). If it is in the root (the same place as your homepage HTML file) and called favicon.ico, you don't need any code. If it isn't, or if you want different favicons for different pages, use this snippet of HTML:

```
<link href="favicon.ico" rel="icon">
```

You can also provide an icon that will be used if someone adds a web page to their iPhone or iPad home screen. It should be 180 x 180 pixels. If it is in the root and called apple-touch-icon.png, you don't need any code. If it isn't, or if you want different icons for different pages, use this:

```
<link href="custom_icon.png" rel="apple-touch-icon">
```

Above: Some examples of home screen icons for websites.

Hot tip

It's best to have just one h1 heading on each page. You can have multiple lower-level headings.

Hot tip

There are special codes to insert symbols. Use © for a copyright sign,   for a non-breaking space (one between two words that you don't want to be on different lines), & for ampersand, < and > for < and >, " for speech marks, and £ for a UK currency symbol. There are also codes for accented letters. Don't forget the semicolon.

Reference: text and forms

Content formatting

HTML tag	Description

`<h1> ... </h1>`
`<h2> ... </h2>`
`<h3> ... </h3>`
	Used to mark up headings. `<h1>` is the most important heading. Headings go down to `<h6>`.

`<p> ... </p>`	Used to mark the start and end of a paragraph.
`<strong> ... </strong>`	Important content, shown by default in bold on screen.
`<em> ... </em>`	Emphasized content, italicized by default.
`<blockquote> ... </blockquote>`	Used to mark up a paragraph-length quote (or longer) or an excerpt from another website.
` `	Line break.
`<hr>`	Horizontal line.

Forms

HTML tag	Description
`<form> ... </form>`	Marks the start and end of a form.
`<label for="id">Label text</label>`	Identifies the label for the form element with a given ID.
`<input type="textbox" id="id" name="name" size="20">`	A one-line textbox that accepts 20 characters. The size is optional. Alternative input types that cannot take a size are radio, checkbox, submit and reset. Other input types include number, password, email, url, tel and date.
`<textarea id="id" name="name" cols="20" rows="5">Default text in the box</textarea>`	A multiline text input box with 20 columns and 5 rows. Anything between these tags becomes the default text in the box.
`<select id="id" name="name"> ... </select>`	Marks the start and end of a select menu. Options go between the tags.
`<option value="value">Option text</option>`	Marks up each option in a select menu.

Reference: tables and lists

Tables

HTML tag	Description
`<table> ...` `</table>`	Marks the start and end of a table.
`<caption>` `...` `</caption>`	Used to indicate a caption for the table, which will appear on screen.
`<th> ...` `</th>`	Marks the start and end of the heading cell for a row or column. If it's ambiguous, indicate whether it is a heading for a row or column by adding a scope attribute to the opening tag: `<th scope="col">` or `<th scope="row">`
`<tr> ...` `</tr>`	Marks the start and end of a table row.
`<td> ...` `</td>`	Marks a table cell. To make the cell span across multiple rows or columns, add a rowspan and/or colspan attribute to the opening tag: `<td rowspan="2">` or `<td colspan="4">`
`<thead> ...` `</thead>`	Marks the head of the table, which should contain the column headings. Multipage table print-outs include the head and foot of the table on each page.
`<tbody> ...` `</tbody>`	Marks the body of the table, which contains the rows of data.
`<tfoot> ...` `</tfoot>`	Marks the foot of the table, which can be used for additional column information.

Bulleted and numbered lists

HTML tag	Description
`<ul> ...` `</ul>`	Defines the start and end of an unordered (bulleted) list.
`<ol> ...` `</ol>`	Defines the start and end of an ordered (numbered) list.
`<li>`	Marks the start of a list item. You can use `</li>` to close a list item, but that is usually unnecessary because the next element is another list item or the end of the list.

Server side includes enable you to share chunks of HTML between different web pages. You could share the header so that you only have one file to update when you add new links to the navbar, for example. There isn't room to cover this technology here, but you can find tutorials online, including on my website.

You can find the full HTML specification at **www.w3.org**

Reference: media and links

Images, audio and video

HTML tag	Description
`<img src="filename.jpg" width="250" height="150" alt="alternative text description here">`	Adds the filename.jpg image to the web page. Specify and width and height to speed up page rendering. The size can also be specified or overridden in CSS.

`<picture>`
`<source media="(min-width: 900px)" srcset="pies-big.jpg">`
`<img src="pies-small.jpg" alt="Home made mince pies">`
`</picture>`
	Specifies different image files for different screen sizes. You can add multiple source media options. The final `<img>` tag is the default image to be used if none of the source media rules apply, or if the `<picture>` tag is not supported by the browser.

`<audio src="music.mp3" controls loop preload="none">`
`<p>Audio is not supported message</p>`
`</audio>`
	Embed a music player that loops the music.mp3 file when the user plays it. To make the audio preload, use `preload="auto"`.

`<video src="video.mp4" controls autoplay muted>`
`<p>Audio is not supported message</p>`
`</video>`
	Embed a video player with controls. To stop autoplay or muted playback, remove those attributes from the tag. You can use the same attributes as for audio: controls, loop, preload.

Links and iframes

HTML tag	Description
`<a href="destination">Link text or image here</a>`	The link destination can be a filename on the current site (e.g. index.html) or a full URL (e.g. https://www.example.com/aboutus.html).
`<iframe src="https://www.example.com/shared/page1.html" name="my_iframe" width="600" height="450">` `</iframe>`	Adds an iframe containing the source web page at example.com. The name can be used as a link target to load other pages into the iframe.

Don't forget

These tags enable you to create sophisticated documents, but this chapter is just a short summary of the most often-used HTML tags. You're not missing anything essential, but as your skills grow, you might want to take a deeper look at the HTML standard.

Hot tip

Add the loading="lazy" attribute to images or iframes so that they only download if the user will see them. This helps to speed up your visitor's experience on your site, and ultimately saves energy by avoiding sending data that will never be seen.

7 CSS: Giving your pages some style

CSS is used to style what your web pages look like, including colors, fonts and layout. In this chapter, you will learn how to style the appearance of your content. You'll also pick up skills you need to experiment with your own designs.

How quickly a web page downloads depends on how many files it has and how large they are in total. Each additional file results in another request to the server, which takes time, in addition to the time taken to download. To speed up a page, minimize the number of different image, style sheet and JavaScript files you use. You can usually put all your CSS code in one file, for example.

You can minify your HTML, CSS and JavaScript, which means taking all the unnecessary spacing out to make files smaller.

Why use CSS?

As you saw in the last chapter, HTML can be used to mark up the structure of your document, but plain HTML looks rather uninspiring. To change the appearance and layout of your document, you use a technique called CSS.

CSS is short for cascading style sheets. The idea is that you put all the instructions for the design of your web page into a separate document called a style sheet. That single style sheet can be shared by lots of different web pages.

It is possible to put style instructions into your HTML file, but it's better to separate your content and design for several reasons:

- When it's time to refresh your site's look, you won't have to trawl through all your HTML files – just update your style sheet, and the design across your whole site will change.

- It's easier to edit your HTML page content, too, because it's not cluttered up with layout and design instructions.

- You can more easily create optimized designs for different devices (such as mobile, desktop and printers). You can use the same HTML for them all.

- Removing the style from your HTML pages makes them smaller, and the style sheet can be cached for use across your site. That means the site will download more quickly because visitors won't need to download the same layout instructions in different web pages.

- If a site degrades gracefully, it means that it still works even if certain browser features aren't available. Your design is more likely to degrade gracefully if you use style sheets and structural HTML. It might not look great on an ancient browser, but it should still work okay.

- Using style sheets makes it easier to enforce a consistent design across a whole web page and a whole website. You can ensure that all your headings look the same, for example, or that all your images have the same border on them.

- Sites occasionally give users a choice of which style sheet to use. They could, for example, change to a dark theme for use at night, or a theme that uses fewer images when on a low-bandwidth connection.

How CSS describes design

Each CSS statement has three elements to it:

- Information about which element of the web page you want to modify the appearance of. This is called the selector. For example, you might use one CSS statement to change all the <h2> headings, or a particular paragraph.

- The name of which detail of that element you want to change. This is called the property. That might be its text color, the border thickness, or the spacing between the element and others on the page.

- Finally, you need to tell the browser what to change that property to – for example, the color red, or a thickness of 4 pixels. We'll call this the value.

You can group CSS statements for the same selectors to save space and to make it easier to understand what's going on. You can also assign the same style rules to as many selectors as you want at the same time. Here's what the CSS syntax might look like if you wanted to change two things about two selectors:

```
selector, selector {
    property: value;
    property: value;
    }
```

As with HTML, you can space out your document however you want. Each rule has to end with a semicolon so that the browser knows when it's finished. If things don't work as expected, first check your semicolons are present and correct.

That looks a bit abstract, so here's a real example. What if you wanted to change your <h1> and <h2> headings so that they have red text and a red line underneath them, like in the illustration below?

Here's the code:

```
h1, h2
{
color: red;
border-bottom: 1px solid
red;
}
```

Beware

The brackets you need are the curled brackets that look like an archery bow {like this}. It won't work if you use the rounded brackets used in written text (like this), or square brackets [like this].

Hot tip

Curious about the Latin in my examples? It's called Lorem ipsum, and it's dummy text used to test layouts. You can find generators online or make it in Word by typing in =lorem(5,5).

107

Hot tip

Note that CSS uses American English spellings – for example, color and center.

First headline h1

Lorem ipsum dolor sit amet, consectetuer adipiscing elit. Maecenas porttitor congue massa. Fusce posuere, magna sed pulvinar ultricies.

Second headline h2

Proin pharetra nonummy pede. Mauris et orci. Aenean nec lorem. In porttitor. Donec laoreet nonummy augue.

Don't forget

I'm using code excerpts here. You'll probably have other things between your <head> tags, too, and that's okay. Just keep them outside your <style> tags.

Hot tip

If there's a conflict, the rule applies that is most specific to a particular element. For example, an inline style trumps a style in the header, which beats a style in an external style sheet. If a style mentions an element by its ID, then that trumps any generic styles applied to all elements of that type.

Adding CSS to your site

The best way to use CSS is to put all your style instructions into a separate text file, called a style sheet. Like HTML documents, style sheets can be written using any text editor. They traditionally have the file extension .css. While you would have one HTML document for each web page on your site, you would only have a few style sheets shared across your site – perhaps only one.

The way that you link your HTML file to your CSS file is to add some code to your HTML document. Unfortunately, you do need to do this for each HTML page of your website. If you had a style sheet called main.css, for example, you would add this line of HTML between the <head> and </head> tags in your web pages:

```
<link rel="stylesheet" href="main.css">
```

There are two other ways you can add style instructions to your website, but I don't recommend you use them often. Both of them make your site harder to manage, because you end up with design instructions spread across lots of different files.

Adding style instructions in the HTML document

The first is to add style instructions between the <head> tags of your HTML document. This might be useful if you had one page on your website with a radically different design for some reason. You put <style> tags around your CSS statements, like this:

```
<head>
    <style>
        h1 {color: red;}
        h2 {color: blue;}
    </style>
</head>
```

Adding style instructions to an HTML tag

You can also add style to a specific HTML tag, known as an inline style. You have to add it to every instance of every tag where you want it to take effect, though.

You could use this to occasionally override a style sheet, but it's better to design the style sheet so that you don't have to. Because you're adding the style to a tag, you don't need to provide a selector. Here's an example of how it works:

```
<h1 style="color: red;">First headline</h1>
```

How to change colors

So far, I've been using the color "red". Red is one of 147 color names that have a standard name in HTML and CSS (representing 140 unique colors). It's a limited palette (see page 111), so designers often choose more specific colors using a number.

What's hexadecimal?

We have 10 fingers and toes, so our number system is based around the number 10 (it's called base 10). Hexadecimal is the kind of counting system we might have if our species had evolved with 16 fingers and toes (base 16). Because we don't have enough number symbols, it uses the letters A to F as well as the digits 0 to 9. When you count in hexadecimal, it looks like this:

0, 1, 2, 3, 4, 5, 6, 7, 8, 9, A, B, C, D, E, F, 10, 11, 12 ... 19, 1A, 1B, 1C, 1D, 1E, 1F, 20, 21, 22 ... 29, 2A, 2B, 2C, 2D, 2E, 2F, 30, 31... 9D, 9E, 9F, A0, A1, A2 ... AE, AF, B0, B1, B2...

It's similar to how we usually count. We keep counting until we've used up all the symbols (including A to F in hexadecimal), and then we increase the next column to the left by one. The numbers don't mean the same thing as they do in our regular number system, though. In our normal number system, 23 means two tens plus three. In hexadecimal, it means two sixteens plus three. The largest two-digit hexadecimal number you can have is FF (which is 255 in base 10).

You don't have to understand how to count in hexadecimal to create a website, but it's useful to be familiar with it. It helps you understand whether one hexadecimal number is bigger than another, and so whether one color is lighter or darker than another. Now you know that you can't have any letters apart from A-F in there, it will also be easier to spot mistakes.

Putting a zero on the front of the number doesn't change the meaning of that number. It does, however, make it easier for the browser to understand where one number ends and another begins. So if you want to use a number that's less than 10, you will usually add a zero to the front of it to make sure that it is still two digits.

For example:

00, 01, 02, 03, 04, 05, 06, 07, 08, 09, 0A, 0B, 0C, 0D, 0E, 0F

Hot tip

There is a shorthand you can use if the red, green, and blue values all use the same digit twice. You only need to use one of them. For example, #F0F is the same as #FF00FF and #369 is the same as #336699.

...cont'd

Hot tip

There is also a CSS property called opacity. Using it, you can set the opacity to a number between 0 and 1 (e.g. 0.5). Applying it to the content box makes the text as well as the background transparent:

div {opacity:0.5;}

Describing colors with hexadecimal

Colors on web pages work a bit like mixing paints. To define a color, you tell the browser how much red, green and blue you want to use, in that order. Each color is measured on a scale that goes from 00 to FF, and they're all combined to create what looks like a single six-digit hexadecimal number but is, in fact, three numbers glued together. A # sign is used in front of it.

So, black – for example – is the absence of any color and so has the number #000000. A vivid red would have as much red as possible (FF), diluted by no green or blue, so it would be #FF0000. If you want to tone the default yellow color down a bit, you could add some blue and, instead of using #FFFF00, use #FFFFCC. Feel free to dabble with the colors.

Changing color

To color the text in an element, you change its color property. The element's background-color property can also be changed:

```
h1 {
    color: #FFFFFF;
    background-color: #008080;
}
```

Using RGBA color numbers

There is another way to specify colors, called RGBA. It's short for red, green, blue and alpha.

RGBA uses three numbers for red, green and blue. In that respect, it's similar to the hexadecimal number system. The difference is that they're your usual (base 10) numbers from 0 to 255.

RGBA is the easiest way to make a transparent color. It features a number between 0 and 1 for the level of opacity (the alpha channel). For example: rgba(255, 0, 0, 1) is solid red; rgba(0, 0, 255, 0.5) is semi-transparent blue. When you use transparency, what's behind can shine through. In this example (right), I've used a background color of rgba(100, 100, 175, 0.5) to create a half-transparent purple box, with a squared paper background showing.

Hot tip

I added that graph paper image (with the filename squares.png) as a background image. Here's the CSS I used:

body {
background-image:
url("squares.png");
}

Find out more

Lorem ipsum dolor sit amet, consectetuer adipiscing elit. Maecenas porttitor congue massa.

...cont'd

Aliceblue (#F0F8FF)	Antiquewhite (#FAEBD7)	Aqua/cyan (#00FFFF)	Aquamarine (#7FFFD4)	Azure (#F0FFFF)	Beige (#F5F5DC)
Bisque (#FFE4C4)	Black (#000000)	Blanchedalmond (#FFEBCD)	Blue (#0000FF)	Blueviolet (#8A2BE2)	Brown (#A52A2A)
Burlywood (#DEB887)	Cadetblue (#5F9EA0)	Chartreuse (#7FFF00)	Chocolate (#D2691E)	Coral (#FF7F50)	Cornflowerblue (#6495ED)
Cornsilk (#FFF8DC)	Crimson (#DC143C)	Darkblue (#00008B)	Darkcyan (#008B8B)	Darkgoldenrod (#B8860B)	Darkgray / darkgrey (#A9A9A9)
Darkgreen (#006400)	Darkkhaki (#BDB76B)	Darkmagenta (#8B008B)	Darkolivegreen (#556B2F)	Darkorange (#FF8C00)	Darkorchid (#9932CC)
Darkred (#8B0000)	Darksalmon (#E9967A)	Darkseagreen (#8FBC8F)	Darkslateblue (#483D8B)	Darkslategray / darkslategrey (#2F4F4F)	Darkturquoise (#00CED1)
Darkviolet (#9400D3)	Deeppink (#FF1493)	Deepskyblue (#00BFFF)	Dimgray / dimgrey (#696969)	Dodgerblue (#1E90FF)	Firebrick (#B22222)
Floralwhite (#FFFAF0)	Forestgreen (#228B22)	Fuchsia (#FF00FF)	Gainsboro (#DCDCDC)	Ghostwhite (#F8F8FF)	Gold (#FFD700)
Goldenrod (#DAA520)	Gray / grey (#808080)	Green (#008000)	Greenyellow (#ADFF2F)	Honeydew (#F0FFF0)	Hotpink (#FF69B4)
Indianred (#CD5C5C)	Indigo (#4B0082)	Ivory (#FFFFF0)	Khaki (#F0E68C)	Lavender (#E6E6FA)	Lavenderblush (#FFF0F5)
Lawngreen (#7CFC00)	Lemonchiffon (#FFFACD)	Lightblue (#ADD8E6)	Lightcoral (#F08080)	Lightcyan (#E0FFFF)	Lightgoldenrodyellow (#FAFAD2)
Lightgray / lightgrey (#D3D3D3)	Lightgreen (#90EE90)	Lightpink (#FFB6C1)	Lightsalmon (#FFA07A)	Lightseagreen (#20B2AA)	Lightskyblue (#87CEFA)
Lightslategray / lightslategrey (#778899)	Lightsteelblue (#B0C4DE)	Lightyellow (#FFFFE0)	Lime (#00FF00)	Limegreen (#32CD32)	Linen (#FAF0E6)
Magenta / fuchsia (#FF00FF)	Maroon (#800000)	Mediumaquamarine (#66CDAA)	Mediumblue (#0000CD)	Mediumorchid (#BA55D3)	Mediumpurple (#9370DB)
Mediumseagreen (#3CB371)	Mediumslateblue (#7B68EE)	Mediumspringgreen (#00FA9A)	Mediumturquoise (#48D1CC)	Mediumvioletred (#C71585)	Midnightblue (#191970)
Mintcream (#F5FFFA)	Mistyrose (#FFE4E1)	Moccasin (#FFE4B5)	Navajowhite (#FFDEAD)	Navy (#000080)	Oldlace (#FDF5E6)
Olive (#808000)	Olivedrab (#6B8E23)	Orange (#FFA500)	Orangered (#FF4500)	Orchid (#DA70D6)	Palegoldenrod (#EEE8AA)
Palegreen (#98FB98)	Paleturquoise (#AFEEEE)	Palevioletred (#DB7093)	Papayawhip (#FFEFD5)	Peachpuff (#FFDAB9)	Peru (#CD853F)
Pink (#FFC0CB)	Plum (#DDA0DD)	Powderblue (#B0E0E6)	Purple (#800080)	Rebeccapurple (#663399)	Red (#FF0000)
Rosybrown (#BC8F8F)	Royalblue (#4169E1)	Saddlebrown (#8B4513)	Salmon (#FA8072)	Sandybrown (#F4A460)	Seagreen (#2E8B57)
Seashell (#FFF5EE)	Sienna (#A0522D)	Silver (#C0C0C0)	Skyblue (#87CEEB)	Slateblue (#6A5ACD)	Slategray / slategrey (#708090)
Snow (#FFFAFA)	Springgreen (#00FF7F)	Steelblue (#4682B4)	Tan (#D2B48C)	Teal (#008080)	Thistle (#D8BFD8)
Tomato (#FF6347)	Turquoise (#40E0D0)	Violet (#EE82EE)	Wheat (#F5DEB3)	White (#FFFFFF)	Whitesmoke (#F5F5F5)
Yellow (#FFFF00)	Yellowgreen (#9ACD32)				

 Hot tip

It doesn't matter whether you use uppercase or lowercase for your hexadecimal digits. I use uppercase because all the symbols are more or less the same size. This helps to spot errors, such as missing digits.

111

Left: The color numbers recognized by CSS, together with their hexadecimal codes. See this chart in your browser at www.sean.co.uk/a/webdesign/css-color-names.shtm

Using gradients

CSS also supports gradients, so you can fade one background color into another. Here's how you create a simple top-to-bottom gradient on your entire web page, fading from purple to yellow (shown below left):

```
body {
    background: linear-gradient(purple, yellow);
}
```

You can change the direction the gradient goes in by specifying an angle, like this (shown below right):

```
body {
    background: linear-gradient(45deg, purple, yellow);
}
```

Using color stops

You can include more than one color to fade between, and you can even specify the points at which you want to color to change. For example, you can say you want the fade to reach the color blue at the 75% point in the space you're coloring:

```
body {
background: linear-
gradient(
    45deg,
    red 10%,
    orange 15%,
    yellow 25%,
    green 45%,
    blue 75%,
    indigo 90%,
    violet 100%
    );
}
```

Changing your fonts

Specifying fonts using CSS is easy. You just need to tell the browser which font-family you want to use. If the font name has a space in it (such as Times New Roman), you put quotes around it. This is how you set your <h2> headings to Times New Roman:

```
h2 { font-family: "Times New Roman"; }
```

You can use the fonts installed on the user's device, which avoids the need to send any fonts over the internet. It's highly efficient, because there are easy-to-read fonts installed on the device already. The challenge is that there are many operating system versions and device types, and they don't all have the same fonts. So, you need to give the browser some choices. Tell it which font you want it to use, but give it some options for if that font isn't available. Finally, if the device doesn't have any of the named fonts you recommend, you can give it some generic font types to use.

The most useful generic types are serif and sans-serif. Serifs are like little ticks of the pen at the end of the strokes on the letters. "Sans" just means without, so a sans-serif font doesn't have those details. Compare the letters S, r, i, b, and d on the right. There is also a monospace generic type, where each character takes up the same amount of space.

You list your font choices in order of preference, like this:

```
h2 { font-family: Calibri,
Geneva, Arial, sans-serif;
}
```

Calibri is included on Windows machines. It's unlikely to be on Apple computers. They will use the next preference Geneva font, which is well established on the Mac (but not on Windows). As our third option, we've specified a super-safe font in Arial. It's available on both Mac and PC, and on many other devices, too. As a last resort, we've requested a sans-serif font if none of our named fonts is available.

Hot tip

If you specify very different fonts, test your website to see how it displays with each of them. Sometimes the spacing of text changes significantly when different fonts are used.

Serif: abcdef
Sans-serif:abcdef

Arial

Comic sans

Courier new

Georgia

Gill Sans

Impact

Palatino

Tahoma

Times New Roman

Trebuchet MS

Verdana

Beware

Using Comic sans is seen as a hallmark of amateur web design by professional web designers.

Left: These fonts are pre-installed on Windows, macOS and Apple mobile devices, but not on Android.

You'll see lots of links to download the fonts from Google, but you don't need to do that. When visitors view your page, the code Google provides will download the fonts from Google's servers. You could put the fonts on your server instead, but you wouldn't benefit from Google's work to ensure each visitor gets the fastest font version that works for them.

You can select multiple Google fonts to add to your website. Each time you select a font, it's a bit like adding it to an order. Google updates your code to include all of your selected fonts in a single request.

Using Google Fonts

Google Fonts provides an easy way to add interesting fonts to your website. Google checks which font formats a browser can use, and sends the smallest file possible to each visitor. It's free.

1 Visit **https://fonts.google.com** in your browser. At the top, you can enter some custom text to test the fonts and can also set the size of the preview text.

2 You can use the **Categories** and **Font Properties** menus to filter the fonts. I'm viewing only the thickest fonts in the screenshot below. You can also choose slanted or wide fonts, and fonts that are serif, sans-serif, handwriting style, monospace or display. Display fonts are designed for use at large sizes.

3 Browse the catalog to find a font you like and select it.

4 The font's page shows you a preview of it at various sizes.

If you have your own custom font, you can create a version for your website using Font Squirrel's Webfont Generator (**https://www.fontsquirrel.com/tools/webfont-generator**). I made a font based on my handwriting for some pages on my site.

5 Click the link to select the font. It's on the right beside your custom text sample.

6 Google gives you code to paste between the <head> tags of your HTML document, and gives you the CSS rules to use the font in your style sheet. The CSS includes a fallback option such as serif, or in this case, cursive.

Use on the web

To embed a font, copy the code into the <head> of your html

⦿ <link>   ○ @import

```
<link rel="preconnect" href="https://
fonts.googleapis.com">
<link rel="preconnect" href="https://
fonts.gstatic.com" crossorigin>
<link href="https://fonts.googleapis.
com/css2?family=Pacifico&display=swa
p" rel="stylesheet">
```

CSS rules to specify families

```
font-family: 'Pacifico', cursive;
```

To make text bold, use the font-weight CSS property. For italics, use font-style. See the reference table at the end of this chapter.

There are four main units of measurement. Pixels are used for line widths, spaces and images. Text is usually sized in rem or em units. They're relative units. 2rem is double the normal font size. 2em is double the size that the text would be, depending on where it is. A 2em paragraph inside a 2em div is four times bigger than the default. You can also use percentages, for if you want a box to take up 30% of the available space, for example.

Padding, border and margin

Every HTML element (including paragraphs, headings, and sections marked up with <div> or <article> tags) has a padding, a border, and a margin. This is known as the box model.

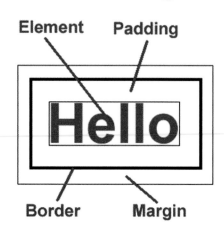

If you had an HTML paragraph that contained the word "Hello", those properties would be arranged around it like this:

This is how the different elements can be used:

● The padding controls how much space there is between the element and its border. You can add padding equally around the element, or you can have uneven padding on the top, bottom, left and right edges. The element's background color stretches to cover the padding too.

● The border is a line on any or all sides of the element. You might add a thin line underneath a heading to create a horizontal rule under it, or you might put a box around a whole section so that it stands out. More often than not, an element has no visible border.

● The margin controls how much space there is between the border and the next element. You can add a margin below a paragraph, for example, to create some empty space before the next paragraph begins. You might put a margin around a picture to offset it slightly from the text.

To set one margin (for example), use the margin-top, margin-bottom, margin-left or margin-right properties. If the margin is the same all the way around, you can use a single value to set it:

```
img { margin: 16px; }
```

To give all four sides different values, list them in the order top, right, bottom, left, like this:

```
img { margin: 0px 8px 16px 8px; }
```

You can use em or rem for sizes, margins and padding so that they change if the user increases the text size.

There are several different border properties you can change:

Property	What it means and example usage
border-width	You can use the values thin, medium or thick, but people usually specify an exact width in pixels. `border-width: 2px;`
border-color	`border-color: black;`
border-style	Describes the border's line: none, solid, dotted, dashed, double, groove, ridge, inset, outset. `border-style: solid;`
border	Used as a shorthand for all those properties, enabling you to combine them into one line. `border: 2px black solid;`

You can change these values for all four sides at once by using those properties in the form shown in the table, or you can specify a particular side (top, bottom, left, right) – for example: border-bottom-width, border-left-color, or border-right-style. The border doesn't have to look the same all the way around.

As an example, let's look at how you can use the border properties to put a red dotted line above and below your <h2> headings, as the screengrab below shows:

```
h2 { border-top: red 2px dotted;
border-bottom: red 2px dotted; }
```

This is a Heading 2

The descender on the letter "g" in that heading looks rather close to the border. What if we wanted to create some extra space between the text and the bottom border, and decided the heading should be indented slightly on the left? This extra CSS for the h2 style declaration would do the trick:

```
padding-left:0.5em; padding-bottom: 0.25em;
```

If you wanted to create some space between the heading and the body copy under it, you could set the margin-bottom property to 1em.

Solid

Dotted

Dashed

Double

Groove

Ridge

Inset

Outset

Above: Border styles.

If you need to change three sides to one value, and the fourth to another, do this: Change all the sides to the most-used value. Then style the odd-one-out. When there is a conflict, the later rule overrides the earlier one. For example:
margin: 1em;
margin-left: 0.5em;

Using CSS selectors

So far, we've seen how to style every occurrence of a particular tag on a page. There are more targeted selectors you can use.

Adding classes to your tags

You can give HTML elements a class name. You can then use that class name in the CSS to select those elements. For example, you might want product photos to have a thick border, but your thumbnail pictures to have a thin one. To do that, you could define two different classes of image. In your HTML, you would add a class definition to your image tag. If you had a class called "thumbnail", for example, your image tag might look like this:

```
<img src="pottery.jpg" width="150" height="50" alt="A
selection of handmade pottery" class="thumbnail">
```

In your CSS, you style class names in a similar way to how you style HTML tags, except that you use a full stop to tell the browser you're referencing a class. For example:

```
.thumbnail {border-width: thin;}
```

Applying more than one class to an element

It is possible to apply more than one class in a tag. You just list all the classes you want to apply in the HTML tag and separate them with a space, like this:

```
<p class="biography sidebar">Biography goes here</p>
```

The browser will then apply the CSS style rules for the classes biography and sidebar.

Selecting by ID

As well as giving an HTML element a class, you can give it an ID. You've already met the ID attribute when creating forms. An ID must be applied only once on each web page, whereas classes can be reused many times on the page. You can choose to use a class just the once, though, so you might not need to use IDs at all. You add an ID to your HTML like this:

```
<div id="advertbox">Advertising goes here</div>
```

To style an ID, use #id, like this:

```
#advertbox {background-color: gray;}
```

tag name
 	
For example:
`h1`
`{font-family: serif;}`
	Selects all instances of that HTML tag. This example sets all h1 headings to use the serif font.

.classname	Selects all HTML elements with the class name. There can be many.
#id	Selects the HTML element with the ID name. There should be only one.
selector, selector For example: `h1, h2 {color: red;}`	Gives the same style rules to multiple selectors. Here, both h1 and h2 headings are colored red.

selector selector
 	
For example:
`header a`
`{text-decoration:`
`none;}`
	Selects all occurrences of the second selector inside the first. The example selects all the <a> tags inside the <header> tag. Setting the text-decoration property to none turns off underlining. This code removes underlining on all header links and no others.

tag.class
 	
For example:
`p.sidebar`
`{color: blue;}`
	Only specific tags with a particular class name are selected. The example turns the text blue in a paragraph with the class name "sidebar", but it ignores any other tags that have that class, and also ignores any <p> tags that do not have that class.

selector > selector
 	
For example:
`div.demos > p`
`{color: red;}`
	Selects elements that are directly inside the first selector. The example turns the paragraphs inside the div with the class name "demos" red. If there's another div inside the "demos" div, any paragraphs inside it aren't selected by this rule.

selector + selector For example: `li + a {color: red;}`	Selects the second selector only if it immediately follows the first.
selector ~ selector For example: `h2 ~ p {color: red;}`	Selects all occurrences of the second selector after the first, with the same parent. For example, all paragraphs after the h2 heading in the same div.

Hot tip

Tags often go inside each other. For example, a link might be inside a paragraph. The inner element is called a child, and the outer one is called a parent.

Hot tip

Don't worry too much about all these selectors. They're here if you need them, but you can do a lot using just tags and class names.

...cont'd

Use ^= to match the start of an attribute and *= to find a word in it. For example, match "grid-box-1" and "grid-box-2" but not "my-grid-box" with:

[class^="grid-box"]

There are some more selectors you can use. For a full description of all the selectors available, see the W3C CSS specification.

tag[attribute*="value"]
 	
For example:
`img[src*="jpg"]`
`{border: 4px red solid;}`
	Selects tags where the named attribute contains the value given. The example here matches all images where the src attribute (the filename) includes jpg, and gives them a red border.

tag:not(.classname)
 	
For example:
`div:not(.new)`
`{color: gray;}`
	Selects instances of a tag that do not have a particular class name. In this case, all divs without the class name "new" have gray text.

selector:has(tag)
 	
For example:
`div:has(img)`
`{border: 8px red solid;}`
	Selects elements with certain other elements inside them. The example here puts a red border on any divs that have an image inside them.

selector:nth-child(number)
 	
For example:
`li:nth-child(2)`
`{font-weight: bold;}`
	Chooses a particular child item in a group. The example here makes the second item in every list bold.

selector:first-child
 	
For example:
`li:first-child`
`{font-weight: bold;}`
	Chooses the first child item. The example here makes the first list item in every list bold.

selector:last-child
 	
For example:
`li:last-child`
`{font-weight: bold;}`
	Chooses the last child item. The example here makes the last list item in every list bold.

selector:nth-child(odd)
 	
For example:
`li:nth-child(odd)`
`{font-weight: bold;}`
	Chooses the odd child items. The example here makes the odd items in every list bold. You can select even instead of odd items.

selector:nth-child(4n)
 	
For example:
`li:nth-child(4n)`
`{font-weight: bold;}`
	Chooses every fourth child item. The example here makes every fourth item in every list bold.

selector:nth-child(4n+2)
 	
For example:
`li:nth-child(4n+2)`
`{font-weight: bold;}`
	Chooses every fourth child item, starting with item 2. The example here makes every fourth item in every list bold, starting with the second list item.

List bullets and numbers

You can give your design some polish by changing the appearance of lists. The default bullets are fine and functional, but lack personality.

For ordered lists, which are usually numbered 1, 2, 3, you can choose, instead, to use roman numerals (uppercase or lowercase) or to use letters (also upper- or lowercase). Generally, it's best to stick with numbers or simple letters because they are most easily understood.

For bullets, there are three different styles. The default is the disc bullet, but you can also choose to use squares or (hollow) circles.

Best of all, you can use your own image as a bullet, so you could have a bullet shaped like your logo, or something linked to the theme of your site. In my example below, I've used musical notes as the bullet. Make sure you use something small and distinctive. The design needs to be simple, otherwise it can distract readers from the content it's supposed to point them toward.

To change the list style between any of the defaults, change the list-style-type CSS property. For example:

```
ul { list-style-type: square; }
ol { list-style-type: upper-alpha; }
```

To use an image for your list instead, you need to specify its path:

```
ul { list-style-image: url(images/notes.gif); }
```

Hot tip

Bulleted lists help people to quickly understand your content.

list-style-type:disc	list-style-type:circle	list-style-type:square
• list item • list item two • list item three	○ list item ○ list item two ○ list item three	▪ list item ▪ list item two ▪ list item three
list-style-type:decimal	**list-style-type:lower-roman**	**list-style-type:upper-roman**
1. list item 2. list item two 3. list item three	i. list item ii. list item two iii. list item three	I. list item II. list item two III. list item three
list-style-type:lower-alpha	**list-style-type:upper-alpha**	**list-style-image: url(notes.gif);**
a. list item b. list item two c. list item three	A. list item B. list item two C. list item three	♪ list item ♪ list item two ♪ list item three

Adding polishing touches

Web designs can seem a bit flat and boxy, but rounded corners in CSS elements can help to soften the design. They're particularly powerful when used for images or content boxes.

Look!
No border!

All rounded corners
The border-radius property enables you to round off the corners on an element. Here's an example usage:

```
border-radius: 100px;
```

Uneven rounded corners
You can specify a different radius for each corner if you wish:

```
border-top-left-radius:
10px;
border-top-right-radius:
30px;
border-bottom-right-
radius: 60px;
border-bottom-left-radius:  90px;
```

As a shorthand, you can give four values for the border-radius property. You start in the top-left corner, and then work your way around clockwise (top-left, top-right, bottom-right, bottom-left):

```
border-radius:  10px  30px  60px  90px;
```

Diagonally symmetrical rounded corners
If you specify just two values for the border-radius property, the first is used for the top left and bottom right, and the second is used for the other two corners:

```
border-radius:  10px  100px;
```

You can also use em or % values to specify the border-radius property. More advanced features of border-radius enable elliptical corners.

Adding text shadows

You can add shadows to a text element to give a sense of depth to it. This can be tiring to read for body text, but works well for headings and for other small chunks of text. The CSS to add a shadow to text looks like this:

```
text-shadow: 8px 8px 0px lightgray;
```

Here's what it looks like, using Google's Monoton font:

The four values are:

- **The horizontal offset for the shadow.** Use a positive number for a shadow to the right, and a negative one for a shadow on the left.

- **The vertical offset for the shadow.** Positive numbers are below the element and negative numbers are above it.

- **The amount of blur on the shadow.** Use 0 for a crisp shadow. Higher numbers give fuzzier shadows.

- **The final value is the shadow color.** I've used a color name here, but you can specify a color number instead.

Adding box shadows

There is also a property you can use to add a shadow to a whole element, such as a div. It is called box-shadow, and uses the same four values as text-shadow. It can make boxes of text appear to pop out of the page.

For example:

```
box-shadow: 8px 8px 8px
lightslategray;
```

This gives the result shown in the image on the right.

You can use text-shadow to make 3D text for viewing with red/green 3D glasses. There is a tutorial at www.sean. co.uk/a/webdesign/3d/ css-text-shadow-anaglyph.shtm

123

Creating a simple navbar

- Home
- Reviews
- Photos
- Music links

Above: This is what the list of links looks like before any CSS is applied. I've set the body's background color to skyblue.

Hot tip

If you want to change the appearance of all the links in your document, just use:
a { *css styles;* }
To change the appearance of visited links, use:
a:visited { *css styles;* }

Hot tip

The :hover and :active parts of the selector are two examples of what are called pseudo-classes.

You can use CSS to turn a list of links into a set of navigation buttons. CSS enables you to offer visual feedback to the website visitor so that they can see which link they are selecting, too.

1 If the style sheet isn't supported or available, your navigation would still make sense as a list of links. Add an unordered list of links to your HTML. Put your navigation links between your <nav> tags. Your HTML should look like this:

```
<nav>
<ul>
        <li><a href="index.html">Home</a>
        <li><a href="reviews.html">Reviews</a>
        <li><a href="photos.html">Photos</a>
        <li><a href="music.html">Music links</a>
</ul>
</nav>
```

2 There are two main types of elements in HTML: block-level and inline. Block-level elements are those that start on a new line. They often contain inline elements. Block-level elements include <p>, <div>, <table> and headings. The unordered list is a block-level element, so we need to change our list items to display inline so that our buttons appear beside each other. Add this line to your CSS:

```
nav li {display: inline;}
```

3 When viewed in your web browser, you should now see your links appear side by side without any bullets. To make these links look like buttons, style them with padding and a border:

```
nav a {
        font-family: arial, sans-serif;
        padding: 8px; margin: 4px;
        color: white;
        background-color: mediumaquamarine;
        border-style: outset;
        border-radius: 8px;
}
```

4 To remove the underlining on the link text, set the text-decoration property to none. Add this rule to your CSS for nav a:

```
text-decoration: none;
```

Web designers often use links in a list like this, but this also works without the list markup and styles.

5 You can specify different or additional style rules that apply when the user is hovering over the link, or focused on it using the keyboard. To create a mouseover effect that shows the user when they are hovering over a link, or have selected it using the keyboard, add the following CSS. It changes the border from outset to inset (which looks like a button being pressed), and also changes the button's background color to turquoise. I've slightly changed the position of the text to make it look more like the button is being pressed in:

```
nav a:hover,
nav a:active
{
        border-style: inset;
        background-color: turquoise;
        position: relative;
        left: 2px;
        top: 2px;
}
```

You can't change the size of an inline element (which a link is). If you want to change the size of your buttons, set your links to be inline blocks. Add these lines to your nav a CSS:

display: inline-block;
width: 8em;

It's a good idea to use em for the width of the button because if the user increases the text size, the button size will increase, too.

6 Test your navbar. You should see that when you put the mouse over it, or when you use the **Tab** key to select it with the keyboard, the button changes.

Home   Reviews   Photos   Music links

7 Experiment! There are lots of different ways you can style a navbar using this basic HTML and CSS.

Transitions and animations

When you use a hover effect, you can make it fade in. Here's how:

Slow transitions like this are rarely a good user experience. Subtle transitions of 0.3 or 0.5 seconds can make an interface feel slicker, though.

I've made this transition unmissable for testing purposes. You probably don't want a transition as extreme as this on a real website, though, with the text size and button size increasing massively.

Animations are fun to make, but don't always make for a great user experience.

1 Here's the HTML I'm using for this example:

```
<a href="#" class="transition_link">Transition test</a>
```

2 Style it using this CSS code:

```
.transition_link
    {
    font-family: arial, sans-serif;
    padding: 8px; margin: 4px;
    color: white; background-color: red;
    border-style: outset; border-radius: 8px;
    text-decoration: none;
    width: 8em;
    display: inline-block;
    font-size: medium;
    }
```

3 Now, add the CSS for the hover effect:

```
.transition_link:hover
    {
    color: red; background-color: white;
    width: 16em;
    font-size: xx-large;
    }
```

4 Try this in your browser. When you hover over the link, the button gets wider, the font grows, and the colors change instantly.

5 Add this line to your .transition_link CSS. It sets the transition between the two states to take 2 seconds:

```
transition: 2s;
```

6 Try it in your browser to see the link gradually change when your mouse cursor rolls over the link and rolls off of it again. If you put the transition property on the hover CSS, the gradual change doesn't happen when the mouse rolls off the link.

Adding animations

You can add automatic animations and set them to repeat. This example flies a butterfly around the screen.

1 Here's the HTML I'm using for this example. That strange code is for the butterfly emoji. Find other emoji codes at **https://emojipedia.org/**

```
<p id="butterfly">&#x1F98B;</p>
```

2 This CSS sets the starting size and position for the butterfly ID. It also binds this CSS to the animation name "flight", and sets the animation to run infinitely. You could change this to a number (e.g. 3) to make it run a set number of times. I've set each complete sequence to take 10 seconds:

```
#butterfly {
       font-size: 100pt;
       transform: rotate(45deg);
       position: absolute;
       top: 50px; left: 50px;
       animation-name: flight;
       animation-duration: 10s;
       animation-iteration-count: infinite;
       }
```

3 Now, you create the "flight" animation CSS. You specify keyframes, which are points in the animation where something changes. You can change many properties at the same time. I'm just changing the position and the font-size property:

```
@keyframes flight{
      33%   {left: 500px;}
      66%   {top: 350px; font-size: 180pt;}
      100% {left: 50px; top: 50px;
               font-size: 100pt;}
      }
```

4 Open the page in your browser. You should see the butterfly move in a triangular pattern.

The butterfly starts and ends its moves slowly. This is using a timing function called "ease". You can change it to linear (same speed throughout), ease-in or ease-out. There is also ease-in-out, which is similar to ease but ease starts faster. Add CSS like this to #butterfly:

animation-timing-function: linear;

I'm using the transform property here to rotate the butterfly emoji.

127

Do you need fancy positioning? You can put a margin around a div or an image, which often eliminates the need for relative positioning.

Hot tip

If you use position:fixed; the element you position will not move when the page scrolls. It stays on the screen as other content scrolls under it.

To make your navbar stick to the top of the screen, with the content scrolling under it, the best approach is:

```
nav {
position: sticky;
top: 0px;
}
```

Advanced positioning

Most of the time, you want your page layout to flow and respond to the screen space available. (We'll explore that more in the next chapter.) You don't need to worry too much about exactly where things will appear.

Sometimes, you might want to position something precisely, on the screen or within a content box. There are two different ways you can position elements using CSS: relatively and absolutely.

- When you position something relatively, you tell the browser where you want it to go, compared to where the browser was going to put it anyway.

- When you position something absolutely, you tell the browser exactly where it should go. This is usually measured from the top left of the browser window. There is an exception: if the element you're positioning is inside something else that has been positioned, then the element you are positioning is measured from that instead. This matters if you are positioning an image that is inside a div and the div has been absolutely positioned, for example.

With either approach, you typically give the browser an offset value from the top and from the left, like this:

```
.productimg
{ position: absolute; top: 20px; left: 20px; }
```

```
.productimg
{ position: relative; top: 15%; left: 35%; }
```

You can also position things from the bottom and the right. This could be used to position something in the bottom-right corner of the screen:

```
position: absolute;
bottom: 2em;
right: 2em;
```

Other ways to specify positions

You can also use negative values. If you want to place something 50 pixels to the left using relative positioning, set a left offset of -50px. In the same way, a negative offset for the top places something above its usual position.

Percentage positioning

One thing to look out for: if you use a percentage for positioning, it is calculated relative to the containing block. If you're relatively positioning an image inside a div using percentages, for example, they will be calculated according to the width and height of the div, and not the image.

Specifying how things overlap

You can end up with elements positioned on top of each other if you use absolute or relative positioning.

By default, those that are added later will appear on top. But you can change which elements appear to be on top of which other elements by setting a value for the z-index property.

This describes the third dimension (depth), and elements with higher values appear to be on top of those with lower values. You set the z-index property, like this:

```
.productimg { z-index: 5; }
```

When you set the size of an element, that doesn't usually include its border and padding. That can make positioning tricky! To make the size include the border and padding, use the box-sizing property on the element, like this:

box-sizing: border-box;

The <table> tag and some of the form elements use the border-box model by default.

129

Left: Three overlapping images, placed using absolute positioning. They were added to the page in the order left to right.

Left: Those same images with z-index values of 10, 5 and 0 applied (from left to right).

At this stage, you might have lots of content boxes joined together. You'll see how to lay out your content boxes in Chapter 8.

Hot tip

The HTML on this page includes Google's code to download the Pacifico font, which the CSS will use.

Creating content boxes

Now, you can style your page content. Here's an example content box I've created. As plain HTML, it looks like the image on this page. The styled page uses the following:

- A transparent color for the article container box.

- Rounded corners on the content box, image and button.

- CSS to change the link to look like a button.

- Google's Pacifico font for the h2 heading.

Here's my HTML:

```
<!DOCTYPE html>
<html lang="en">
<head>
<title>Content box design test</title>
<link rel="stylesheet" href="main.css">
<link rel="preconnect" href="https://fonts.googleapis.
com">
<link rel="preconnect" href="https://fonts.gstatic.
com" crossorigin>
<link href="https://fonts.googleapis.com/css2?family=P
acifico&display=swap" rel="stylesheet">
</head>
<body>
<article>
    <h2>Scratch Programming in easy steps</h2>
    <img src="images/books.jpg" alt="A stack of
copies of Scratch Programming in Easy Steps">
    <p class="description">Discover how to:</p>
    <ul>
        <li>Build exciting games</li>
        <li>Use a Sense HAT and webcam</li>
        <li>Create stunning visual effects</li>
    </ul>
    <p><a href="shop.html" class="orderbutton">Order
now!</a></p>
</article>
</body>
</html>
```

Here's the CSS I wrote to style that content as shown on this page. I've put the rules in the order they apply, from top to bottom of the web content. This makes it easier to find the rules to edit in the CSS later.

```
body {
padding: 32px;
background-image:
url('images/squares.png');
color: black; }

article{
width: 416px;
background-color:
rgba(255, 228, 196, 0.6);
padding: 0 16px 16px
16px;
border-radius: 16px; }

article h2{
font-family: 'Pacifico', cursive;
font-size: 2.5rem;
padding-top: 8px;
border-bottom: 4px goldenrod dotted;
text-shadow: 2px 2px 2px goldenrod;
color: black; }

article img {
border-radius: 16px; }

article p, article ul li {
font-size: 1.75rem;
font-family: 'Gill Sans', 'Gill Sans MT', Calibri,
'Trebuchet MS', sans-serif }

article ul {
margin-bottom: 32px;
list-style-type: circle;
}

.orderbutton {
text-decoration: none;
background-color: chocolate;
color: white;
padding: 16px;
border-radius: 8px; }
```

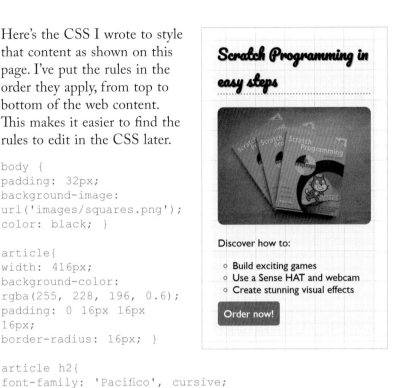

I put these style instructions into a file called main.css. It's linked between the <head> tags of the HTML file.

You can check the quality of your CSS using the W3C validator at http://jigsaw.w3.org/css-validator/

Experiment! You can use a piece of code as short as this HTML (a heading, an image, a paragraph, a list, and a link) to test lots of CSS design ideas quickly.

Hot tip

You can, of course, also make the box float to the right. Remember to adjust the margins so that the box lines up with the right edge of the text and has space between it and the text on the left:

float: right;
margin: 0px 0px 8px 8px;

Hot tip

You don't have to use a div. You could float a content box like the one on page 131. Give its article tag a class, and set it to float.

Don't forget

The margin values are specified in the following order: top, right, bottom, left. The order is clockwise.

Floating content boxes

You can create a simple layout by floating a content box or image so that text flows around it. This is useful for laying out boxes of related information, such as requirements at the top of a tutorial.

 1 Here's my HTML. I've left out most of the text here:

```
<div class="instructions">
    <h1>How to build a chicken coop</h1>
    <div class="floatbox">
        <h2>What you need:</h2>
        <ul>
            <li>First item is most important
            <li>Second item goes here
            <li>Third item in the list
            <li>Fourth item sits here
            <li>Fifth item is this one
        </ul>
    </div>
    <p>First paragraph.</p>
    <p>Second paragraph.</p>
    <p>Third paragraph.</p>
</div>
```

2 To make the box float to the left, use float: left as shown here. The margins define the space between the box and the text outside it. I've set the margins to 8px on the bottom and right, and 0 at the top and left so that the box lines up with the top and left of the main text:

```
.floatbox{
    float: left;
    margin: 0px 8px 8px 0px;
}
```

How to build a chicken coop

What you need:

- First item is most important
- Second item goes here
- Third item in the list
- Fourth item sits here
- Fifth item is this one

Lorem ipsum dolor sit amet, consectetuer adipiscing elit. Maecenas porttitor congue massa. Fusce posuere, magna sed pulvinar ultricies, purus lectus malesuada libero, sit amet commodo magna eros quis urna.

Nunc viverra imperdiet enim. Fusce est. Vivamus a tellus.

Pellentesque habitant morbi tristique senectus et netus et malesuada fames ac turpis egestas. Proin pharetra nonummy pede. Mauris et orci.

Aenean nec lorem. In porttitor. Donec laoreet nonummy augue.

Suspendisse dui purus, scelerisque at, vulputate vitae, pretium mattis, nunc. Mauris eget neque at sem venenatis eleifend. Ut nonummy.

Lorem ipsum dolor sit amet, consectetuer adipiscing elit. Maecenas porttitor congue massa. Fusce posuere, magna sed pulvinar ultricies, purus lectus malesuada libero, sit amet commodo magna eros quis urna.

Reference: text formatting

Property	Valid values
font-family	A list of named fonts. If font names have more than one word, enclose them in quotes. A generic type: serif / sans-serif / monospace / cursive / fantasy
font-size	A percentage: for example, 150%. An em or rem value: for example, 3em or 2rem. A size description: xx-small / x-small / small / medium / large / x-large / xx-large.
font-style	italic / normal
font-weight	bold / normal / lighter / bolder
font	This is a shorthand way of formatting fonts. For example: `p {font: bold italic Palatino, serif}`
text-align	left / right / center / justify
text-indent	An em value: for example, 3em. A percentage: for example, 5%. Sets an indent for the first line of text.
text-transform	capitalize / uppercase / lowercase / none You can use this setting to change the case of text. capitalize puts the first character of each word into uppercase. The uppercase and lowercase values change all characters.
color	A color number or name; e.g. #FF0000 or red.
list-style-type	disc / circle / square / decimal / lower-roman / upper-roman / lower-alpha / upper-alpha
list-style-image	Path to your image. For example: `ul { list-style-image: url(dot.gif); }`
text-decoration-style	solid / double / dotted / dashed / wavy Sets the type of line used for text-decoration. Text decoration is usually used for links.
text-decoration	underline / overline / line-through / none You can also set a color: `text-decoration: underline red;`

Hot tip

An em or % font-size is relative to its current size, and not necessarily relative to the default size. If a div has a font-size of 150%, and a paragraph in it has a font-size of 200% applied to it, the text in the paragraph will be twice as large as the rest of the div content, which will be one and a half times as large as text content outside the div. To avoid unintended effects, use rem instead of em.

Beware

Font size is often measured in points (pt) in applications like word processing. You can set an absolute size for text (e.g. 12pt or 32px) on your website, but it's best not to. It stops the user from being able to adjust the text size to their preferences.

Reference: backgrounds

Property	Valid values
background-color	A color number or name; e.g. #FF0000 or red.
background-image	url(path to image file). You can specify multiple (semi-transparent) background images, and separate them with commas. Example: `body{background-image: url(train.jpg);}`

background-position	One or more word values:
	top / bottom / right / left / center
	
	Two measurements for how far from the left and top of the element the background should start. For example, 8px 16px.
	
	Two percentages for the x and y position; e.g. 10% 20%. This would place the point that is 10% across and 20% down the image, at the point that is 10% across and 20% down the element that the background is in. A value of 0% 0% aligns the background with the top-left corner of the element. 100% 100% aligns it with the bottom-right corner.
	
	Example:
	`body {background-position: 8px 16px; }`
	`body {background-position: top center; }`
	`body {background-position: 30% 50%; }`

background-attachment	fixed / scroll This property dictates whether the background scrolls with the element's content or stays fixed.
background-repeat	repeat / repeat-x / repeat-y / no-repeat This property dictates whether the background image is repeated. repeat-x and repeat-y enable you to limit the repetition to the horizontal or vertical direction.

background	A shorthand property for the other background properties. For example:
	`.trainpara {`
	`background: url("train.jpg") black`
	`repeat fixed;}`

Beware

If you use a background image, make sure you also set a background color that contrasts with the foreground color. Otherwise, your text might be unreadable when the image is not available.

Don't forget

For a reference to selectors, see pages 119-120.

Reference: spacing, borders

Spacing

Property	Valid values
margin	auto A measurement or percentage; e.g. 8px or 30%. The percentage margin applied to an element is calculated according to the size of its container, and not the size of the element itself. For example, if a div with a class of .article is inside a div with a class of .wrapper and has a right margin of 20%, its right margin will be 20% of the width of .wrapper. Different values can be set for margin-top, margin-bottom, margin-left and margin-right.
padding	A measurement or percentage, calculated based on the containing element (see notes for margin, above). Different values can be set for padding-top, padding-bottom, padding-left and padding-right.
line-height	A number to be multiplied by the font size (e.g. 1.5).
letter-spacing	A measurement of spacing between letters. Negative values can be used to close the default gap; e.g. 1.5em or -1.5em. Avoid large values.
word-spacing	As for letter-spacing, above, but it applies to spaces between words.

Borders

Property	Valid values
border-width	thin / medium / thick Width in pixels, such as border-width: 2px;
border-color	A color number or name; e.g. #FF0000 or red.
border-style	none / solid / dotted / dashed / double / groove / ridge / inset / outset
border	Used as a shorthand for all those properties, enabling you to combine them into one line. Example: `.wrapper { border: 2px black solid; }`

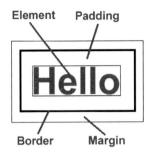

Above: The box model shows how padding, margins, and borders apply to an element.

Set the left and right margins to auto to center the element.

Browsers apply different default margins and padding, which can lead to inconsistent layouts. To remove all padding and margins on everything, you can start your style sheet with:

```
* {padding: 0;
    margin: 0; }
```

Reference: presentation

Hot tip

To help you remember what your CSS does, you can add comments in it, like this:

/*This is a comment*/

Comments are ignored by the browser. To disable a chunk of CSS temporarily, while you experiment, turn it into a comment:

/* float: right; margin-left: 8px; */

Submit form!

Above: Using a linear-gradient for a colorful background on an input button, together with a text shadow for the text on the button.

Property	How it is used
border-radius	Specifies how rounded the corners on an element should be. If you provide four values, they are used for the top left, top right, bottom right, and bottom left in that order. If two values are provided, the first one is for the top left and bottom right, and the second is for the other two corners. If one value is provided, it applies to all four corners. Example: `border-radius: 8px 2px 12px 4px;`
text-shadow	Adds a drop shadow to text. The four values provided are the horizontal offset (negative number is left, positive is right); the vertical offset (negative number is up, positive is down); the amount of blur; and the shadow color. Example: `text-shadow: 2px 2px 8px gray;`
box-shadow	This property adds a shadow to an element, such as a box of text or an image. It uses the same values as text-shadow, above. Example: `box-shadow: 2px 2px 2px black;`
opacity	The opacity property determines how transparent an element is. The value goes from 1 (which is opaque, or normal) to 0 (which is so transparent it's invisible). Example: `opacity: 0.75;`

linear-gradient	You can fade background colors into each other, like this:
	
	`background: linear-gradient(45deg, purple, yellow);`
	
	You can specify the points where colors should change, like this:
	
	`background: linear-gradient(red 10%, orange 50%, yellow 75%);`

Reference: position and size

Position

Property	Valid values
float	left / right
clear	left / right / both Specifies on which side of an element floating is not allowed.

position	absolute / relative
	Uses a measurement for the offset to the right and down. Negative numbers are valid. Absolute positions are relative to the top-left corner of the screen unless inside another positioned element. Relative positions are compared to where the element would normally have been on the page.
	
	Examples:
	`position: absolute; top:20px; left:20px;`
	`position: relative; top:15%; left:35%;`

z-index	A number. When elements overlap, the z-index property determines which is in front. Higher numbers are in front of lower numbers. You can set negative values.
overflow	visible / hidden / clip / scroll / auto Determines what happens to excess content – for example, if the size of a box is set using a fixed width and height and the text doesn't fit. This can often be avoided by sizing elements containing text using em measurements.

Size

Property	Valid values
width	A measurement or percentage; e.g. 8px, 30em or 70%. The percentage width is specified relative to the containing element. For example, imagine a div that has a width of 70% and is the first object in the body. The div will have the width of 70% of the body.
height	A measurement or percentage; e.g. 8px, 30em or 70%. See notes for width, above.

Hot tip

You don't have to use all of these properties. The width and height, for example, are automatically calculated, unless you specify them.

Hot tip

You can stop a paragraph flowing around floated content. For a paragraph with a class of "para", use:

.para { clear: both; }

Hot tip

There are also CSS properties of min-width, max-width, min-height and max-height, which set the minimum and maximum desired dimensions.

Pseudo-classes and elements

Pseudo-classes enable you to attach conditions to using a selector. For example, you can set a style to apply only when a link has been visited.

This chapter doesn't cover all the capabilities of CSS. The W3C website (www.w3c.org) has a full list.

Pseudo-elements let you style a part of a selector, such as the first letter. They use two colons, although most browsers also support one for the pseudo-elements here.

Property	How it is used
:active	Used for behavior of links when the user has tabbed to them using the keyboard, or is clicking on them using the mouse.
:hover	Used for behavior when the user is hovering over an element. To make links appear highlighted in yellow when the mouse is over them, use: `a:hover { background-color: yellow; }`
:link	Used to style unvisited links; e.g.: `a:link { color: blue; }`
:visited	Used to style visited links; e.g.: `a:visited { color: purple; }`

:focus	Styles elements when they are accepting text input. For example, to make form fields light blue when they are in use:
	`input:focus, select:focus,`
	`textarea:focus`
	`{ background-color: aliceblue; }`

::first-letter	Used to style the first letter in an element. For example, to enlarge the first letter of each paragraph in any div with a class name of article, use:
	
	`.article p:first-letter`
	`{font-size: 2em;}`

::first-line	Used to style the first line in an element. Usage is the same as for first-letter, above.

::after
::before
	Used to add some text content before or after a particular element. For example, to add the word "Warning" before any paragraph with the class of warning, use:
	`p.warning:before { content: "Warning" ;}`
	
	You can also add an image using its path:
	`p.warning:before {`
	`content: url(warningbox.jpg); }`
	
	This is sometimes used to add an icon beside links. Don't depend on this to add important information to the web page. These pseudo-classes do not work reliably on screen readers.

8 CSS: Using CSS for layout

Your design needs to work on a range of devices and viewport sizes. Here, you'll discover CSS features for laying out pages. They include flexbox and grid, which help you to create responsive websites. I'll also show you how media queries work and how you can create a responsive navbar.

Creating column layouts

In newspapers, text is often split into columns. It's easier to read lots of short lines than a long line that spans the whole page. You can create columns on a web page using these CSS properties:

- **column-count:** How many columns to split the text across.

- **column-gap:** The space between the columns, which is 1em unless you change it.

- **column-rule:** The style of the dividing line between the columns, expressed the same as a border style.

- **column-width:** An optional minimum width for the column.

- **column-span:** Whether you would like your text to span the columns. Valid values are "all" or "none".

Let's see an example:

1 Here's the HTML code I'm styling. I've left out the real content here so that it's easier to see the structure:

```
<div class="columns_div">
      <h1>The title goes here</h1>
      <p>First paragraph.</p>
      <p>Second paragraph.</p>
      <p>Third paragraph.</p>
</div>
```

2 Style the columns like this:

```
.columns_div {
      column-count: 3;
      column-gap: 20px;
      column-rule: 4px white double;
}
```

Beware

If your columns are too deep, readers may have to scroll up and down to read them. Columns are best used for short pieces of text.

Hot tip

There is a shorthand columns property. It combines the column width and the number of columns – for example, columns: 200px 3;

Create digital art on the Raspberry Pi

ArtEvolver is an ever-changing digital artwork that blends together images, constantly changing their transparency. Each time you look at it, you'll see a fresh mix of the images.

For my installation, I've curated a collection of 1,000 images, but you can use maybe 10 to try it out, and get good results with 100 images. Some of the images are my own, and some are from online libraries. I sought out textures (stone, paper, oil paints) and colour gradients, as well as interesting abstract shapes. There is an element of trial and error. Some images didn't work as well as I hoped for, and so I removed them again.

From a technical point of view, the key was working out how to index all the images in Python, which makes it scalable because you can easily add and remove images without changing code. From a reader's point of view, the project has a low barrier to entry while offering potential for self expression. The code is documented but can just be cut and pasted, and customisation is simply a question of sourcing and curating images. The finished installation looks great mounted in a picture frame, but you can run it on the Raspberry Pi desktop without any additional hardware.

3 We can style the heading so it spans across the columns using the column-span property:

```
.columns_div h1 { column-span: all; }
```

Create digital art on the Raspberry Pi

ArtEvolver is an ever-changing digital artwork that blends together images, constantly changing their transparency. Each time you look at it, you'll see a fresh mix of the images.

For my installation, I've curated a collection of 1,000 images, but you can use maybe 10 to try it out, and get good results with 100 images. Some of the images are my own, and some are from online libraries. I sought out textures (stone, paper, oil paints) and colour gradients, as well as interesting abstract shapes. There is an element of trial and error. Some images didn't work as well as I hoped for, and so I removed them again.

From a technical point of view, the key was working out how to index all the images in Python, which makes it scalable because you can easily add and remove images without changing code. From a reader's point of view, the project has a low barrier to entry while offering potential for self expression. The code is documented but can just be cut and pasted, and customisation is simply a question of sourcing and curating images. The finished installation looks great mounted in a picture frame, but you can run it on the Raspberry Pi desktop without any additional hardware.

4 Finally, we can add some paragraph styles to tidy it up and make it easier to see where each paragraph begins. Using the ::first-letter selector, we can style the first letter of each paragraph differently from the rest:

```
p {
        margin: 0px; padding: 0px;
        margin-bottom: 1em;
}

p::first-letter {
        font-weight: bold;
        font-size: 200%;
}
```

Don't forget

You can set the column-span property to all or none. You can't set it to a certain number of columns.

Create digital art on the Raspberry Pi

ArtEvolver is an ever-changing digital artwork that blends together images, constantly changing their transparency. Each time you look at it, you'll see a fresh mix of the images.

For my installation, I've curated a collection of 1,000 images, but you can use maybe 10 to try it out, and get good results with 100 images. Some of the images are my own, and some are from online libraries. I sought out textures (stone, paper, oil paints) and colour gradients, as well as interesting abstract shapes. There is an element of trial and error. Some images didn't work as well as I hoped for, and so I removed them again.

From a technical point of view, the key was working out how to index all the images in Python, which makes it scalable because you can easily add and remove images without changing code. From a reader's point of view, the project has a low barrier to entry while offering potential for self expression. The code is documented but can just be cut and pasted, and customisation is simply a question of sourcing and curating images. The finished installation looks great mounted in a picture frame, but you can run it on the Raspberry Pi desktop without any additional hardware.

Using flexbox

The flexible box layout scheme, known as flexbox, helps to create responsive designs that change depending on the size of the browser window.

In this example, I'll show you how to lay out a series of articles using flexbox. In my demo, each article is represented by an image, but it could be a content box, like the one I made in the last chapter. The images are numbers so that you can easily see how flexbox works.

Above: Flexbox is great for responsive designs. On a mobile phone, the flexbox could show as a single column of articles. On a wide screen, it could be many columns. Remember the meta tag to stop the mobile device resizing the page:

```
<meta
name="viewport"
content="initial-
scale=1.0",
width="device-width">
```

1 Here's my HTML for marking up the content boxes:

```
<div class="articles">
    <article class="number">
        <img src="1.jpg">
    </article>
    <article class="number">
        <img src="2.jpg">
    </article>
    <!-- more articles, up to 8.jpg -->
</div>
```

2 The div that contains all the articles is called "articles". These CSS instructions will make it a flexbox container. Without setting it to wrap, you'll have a row of boxes that stretches off the screen:

```
.articles {
    display: flex;
    flex-wrap: wrap;
}
```

3 Open the page in your browser, and you'll see that the articles tile, from left to right, and top to bottom.

...cont'd

4 When the browser window is narrowed, the layout adjusts. A column is removed on the right, and the boxes tile further down the page.

flex-direction: row-reverse;
reverses the items in the rows, as shown below:

flex-wrap: wrap-reverse reverses the rows, but not the items in them, as shown below:

143

5 You can change the direction of the flow so that boxes tile from top to bottom and then left to right instead. To see this, you need to fix the container height. The height value depends on the size of your images. Here's the CSS you need, changing both the flex-direction property to column (instead of row) and setting the height value:

```
.articles {
     display: flex;
     flex-wrap: wrap;
     flex-direction: column;
     height: 700px;
}
```

Aligning flex items

Use the justify-content property on the flexbox container to tell the browser how to align flexbox items. The possible values are:

- **flex-start:** This is the default. Items are aligned with the start of the flexbox, leaving space on the other side. Assuming your flex direction is row, the space is on the right.

- **flex-end:** This aligns items with the end of the flexbox.

- **center:** This centers items within the flexbox.

- **space-between:** The space between adjacent items is the same. Items fill the flexbox.

- **space-around:** The space around adjacent items is the same. Items are centered in the flexbox.

- **space-evenly:** The space between adjacent items and at the edges is the same.

Don't forget

Apply the justify-content property to the flexbox container, not the items. For example:

.articles
{ display: flex;
flex-wrap: wrap;
justify-content: center; }

Beware

If you change the flex direction, these alignments will work vertically instead of horizontally.

Right: The different flexbox alignment options.

Top row:
flex-start, flex-end

Middle:
center, space-between

Bottom row:
space-around, space-evenly

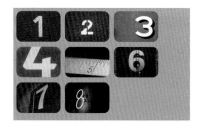

Flexing box sizes

The size of the boxes can adjust to fill the space available by using the flex property on your flexbox items. It takes three values:

- **grow:** The amount of extra space the item can acquire, compared to the others. An item with a grow value of 2 gets twice as much of the free space as an item with a value of 1.

- **shrink:** When there is not enough space for all the items, this value says how much space can be taken away from a flex item. An item with a shrink value of 2 will have twice as much space taken away as one with a value of 1.

- **basis:** This is the starting size of the flex item. If you give the item a shrink value of 0, the basis becomes its minimum size. Unless you use a value of "auto" here, the basis overrides any width or height values on the element.

You can make all items share the free space equally, like this:

```
.number { flex: 1 1 auto; }
```

This might not make all the items the same size. The space on each line is shared equally between the boxes on that line, but there may be more items on some lines, depending on the viewport size.

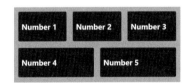

To make some boxes bigger than others, you could use:

```
.number1 { flex: 3 1 100px; }
.number2 { flex: 2 1 100px; }
.number3 { flex: 1 1 100px; }
```

The free space is shared in the proportions in the grow value, as shown below. The first box consumes three times as much free space as box 3. This doesn't make box 1 three times the size of box 3. It's just acquired more free space than box 3 did. (We could alternatively have used the one-value forms of flex 3, flex 2 and flex 1 if we didn't need to set the 100px basis size.)

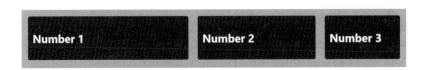

Don't forget

Give each item a unique class to style it separately. Items can have more than one class:

<article class= "number number4">

Hot tip

You can change the order of flexbox items:

.number4 {order: 3;}

Give an order for each item. Items without an order value come after negative order numbers and before positive ones.

Hot tip

The flex-flow property is a shorthand for the flow direction and wrapping:

flex-flow: column wrap-reverse;

Although this is a simple demo, we could have used any style instructions. This code could be the framework for a sophisticated responsive website.

You can also test the device orientation. Use (orientation: landscape) or (orientation: portrait) in your media query.

Don't try to design for every device. In some cases, it's enough to design for mobile devices and add instructions for devices with more than 600 pixels of width.

Using media queries

Media queries enable you to check the characteristics of the device viewing the web page, and then set different CSS styles. Typically, media queries are used to cater for different screen sizes.

You can use media queries to direct style instructions to devices with a screen and a particular minimum and maximum width. For example, you can target phones by default, and then add different rules for devices between 600 and 992 pixels wide (tablets and large phones), for devices 992 to 1200 pixels wide (laptops and desktops), and for ultra-wide devices more than 1200 pixels wide.

 Enter this HTML and CSS in your editor and save it:

```
<!DOCTYPE html>
<html lang="en">
<head>
<meta charset="utf-8">

<style>
body {border: 64px red outset; height: 500px;}

@media screen and (min-width: 600px) and
(max-width: 992px) {
      body {border: 64px orange outset;}
         }

@media screen and (min-width: 992px) and
(max-width: 1200px) {
      body {border: 64px yellow outset;}
         }

@media screen and (min-width: 1200px) {
      body {border: 64px green outset;}
         }
</style>

</head>
</html>
```

2 Open that web page in your browser. The page is blank, except for the colored border.

3 Resize the browser window horizontally. As the window width changes, the different style rules will apply and the border color of the page body tag will change.

Printer-friendly pages

Have you ever printed a web page, only to find that the end of each line is missing and you have three extra pages of adverts and navigational images that make no sense on paper? Don't let this happen on your website! CSS offers the perfect solution.

1 At the end of your usual style sheet, add the media code to enclose your print styles:

```
@media print {
               }
```

2 Identify any sections of the page that shouldn't be printed. That might include adverts or entire sidebars or navigation sections. For each one, add a style declaration to stop them displaying, inside your print media brackets:

```
@media print {
        nav { display: none; }
        .advertbox { display: none; }
        }
```

3 Check for any style declarations that won't work in print. Background colors and pictures don't print, so change any colors that won't contrast well with white paper:

```
@media print {
        nav { display: none; }
        .advertbox { display: none; }
        .codebox { color: black; }
        }
```

4 If there's something you'd like to suppress from printing that is not already marked up in a way you can easily target in your CSS, you might need to add <div> and </div> tags around it in your HTML. Give the opening tag a class of something like do_not_print:

```
<div class="do_not_print"> ... </div>
```

5 When you've marked up the HTML, set the marked-up divs to not print by adding this to your print CSS rules:

```
.do_not_print { display: none; }
```

Try printing (or even just print previewing) a number of pages on your site, representing different types of content. That will help you to ensure you catch anything that might frustrate visitors.

147

In the same way you have content that only appears on screen, you can add a footer that only appears on print-outs. Just wrap it in a div with a class name like print_only and then set that to not display on screen:

```
@media screen {
.print_only
{display: none;}
}
```

Creating a responsive navbar

Now you've learned how to use media queries and flexbox, you can combine them to make a responsive navbar.

It renders as a column of links on a mobile phone or narrow browser window, and as a single row of links on bigger devices or windows, such as on desktop and laptop computers.

Hot tip

You can make the navbar smaller, but make sure it remains big enough for people to tap comfortably.

1 Here's the HTML for the navbar. You can change the links in it, and add more if you need them:

```
<nav>
        <a href="index.html">Home</a>
        <a href="reviews.html">Reviews</a>
        <a href="photos.html">Photos</a>
        <a href="music.html">Music</a>
</nav>
```

2 Between your <head> and </head> tags, add this meta tag. It stops mobile phones resizing the web page. The iPhone will otherwise show the desktop navigation for the user to zoom in, and not the mobile navbar designed for phones:

```
<meta name="viewport"
content="width=device-width, initial-scale=1.0">
```

3 Style your navbar for mobile. The nav element is a flexbox container for the links. The styles for the links remove the underlining and put a border underneath each link:

```
nav {
        display: flex;
        flex-wrap: wrap;
        flex-direction: column;
        background-color: #FFF73B;
}

nav a {
        color: black;
        font-family: arial;
        text-decoration: none;
        font-weight: bold;
        font-size: xx-large;
        padding: 16px;
        border-bottom: 1px black dashed;
        text-align: center;
}
```

Above: The navbar so far, as seen in the iPhone browser.

4 The navbar doesn't quite touch the edges of the browser window, because of padding on the body tag. To make the navbar hug the edge of the browser, add the following instruction:

```
body { margin: 0px; }
```

5 Let's add a hover action so that the navbar buttons light up when they are hovered over or activated:

```
nav a:hover,
nav a:active
        { background-color: #f0f0f0; }
```

Phones can't detect a finger hovering over a link. Computer users might view your web page in a narrow window, though, so I've set the hover action in the default styles, not just in those for wider devices. You might prefer not to add hover styles for mobile devices.

6 Now the navbar is complete for mobile devices, let's design the styles to be used on wider devices. I've decided to apply these styles to browser windows wider than 600 pixels. The styles change the flex-direction property from column to row, and justify (or align) the content on the right:

```
@media screen and (min-width: 600px)
{
        nav{
                justify-content: right;
                flex-direction: row;
        }

        nav a {
                border: none;
                border-right: 1px black dashed;
        }
}
```

7 Open the web page in your browser with a wider window to see the horizontal navbar.

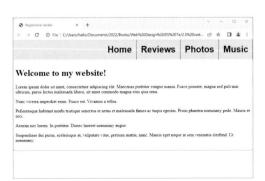

Add some padding or margin to your main page content, to stop it sitting against the edge of the browser window.

Creating your first grid

Although flexbox can enable rows and columns, a CSS grid is a better way to lay out web content in two dimensions. You can change where something sits on the grid and can manage the layout in rows and columns at the same time.

Hot tip

For really complicated layouts, you can put a flexbox inside a grid, or a grid inside a flexbox. You can put a grid inside a grid, too, or a flexbox inside a flexbox.

1 To create a grid, you need a containing element and a set of grid items. Here's some simple HTML to get started:

```
<div class="grid_container">
        <div class="grid-box-1">1 LOGO</div>
        <div class="grid-box-2">2 NAVBAR</div>
        <div class="grid-box-3">3 SIDEBAR</div>
        <div class="grid-box-4">4</div>
        <div class="grid-box-5">5</div>
        <div class="grid-box-6">6</div>
        <div class="grid-box-7">7</div>
        <div class="grid-box-8">8</div>
        <div class="grid-box-9">9</div>
</div>
```

2 Let's style each div inside the grid container so that we can see its boundaries. I've given each grid box a double-lined black border, and I've set the color and size of the text so that we can easily see which grid boxes are where. This will matter when we move them around later:

```
.grid_container > div {
        border: 4px black double;
        font-family: sans-serif;
        font-size: 32px;
        color: red;
}
```

Don't forget

Using > selects elements that are directly inside the first selector. Here, we select all the divs that are directly inside .grid_container.

3 Now, let's set up the grid. We style the grid container by setting its display property to grid. We define three columns, which are 100px, 200px, and 300px wide. We also define three rows, which are 100px, 200px and 300px high. We set the gap between the grid items at 20px:

```
.grid_container{
        display: grid;
        grid-template-columns: 100px 200px 300px;
        grid-template-rows: 100px 200px 300px;
        grid-gap: 20px;
}
```

4 Open your web page in your browser. It looks like this:

5 Try adding some more grid box divs inside your container div. I've added grid-box-10 and grid-box-11 using code similar to Step 1 on the previous page.

6 Save your web page and refresh it in your browser. The new boxes are added to a new row on your existing grid. The browser makes its best guess of how to size these boxes. We'll fix that shortly so that they match the others.

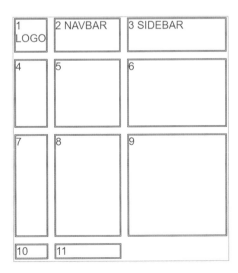

When you're creating a new design, add borders or colored backgrounds to your content boxes so that you can easily see their boundaries.

Managing larger grids

Let's explore the options for dealing with larger grids, or grids with an unknown number of grid boxes.

1 Using repeat() you can avoid writing out the width of identical columns or rows over and over again. For example, repeat(3, 300px) stands in for 300px 300px 300px. You can use repeat together with other values in a row or column, too. We can make one row of 100px followed by two of 300px, for example:

```
.grid_container{
        display: grid;
        grid-template-columns: repeat(3, 300px);
        grid-template-rows: 100px repeat(2,
                300px);
        grid-gap: 20px;
}
```

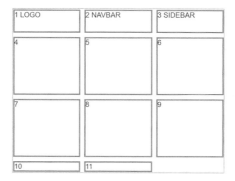

2 Those extra boxes 10 and 11 are still sized for their content. We could have changed our grid-template-rows property to include them, but the grid-auto-rows property enables us to set the size of any row that's added. Add this line to the CSS for your grid_container div:

```
grid-auto-rows: 300px;
```

3 Save your web page and refresh it in your browser. You should see that boxes 10 and 11 are the same size as the row above. You can add more boxes in your HTML, and they will also be 300px high.

4 By default, grid items are organized from left to right, top to bottom. Additional grid items appear in new rows. You can make grid items run from top to bottom, left to right, with new items in new columns instead. Add this line in the CSS for your grid_container div:

```
grid-auto-flow: column;
```

5 Save your web page and refresh it in your browser. Boxes 10 and 11 now start a new column on the right, instead of starting a new row underneath the defined grid. Notice also how the box numbers now run in columns, not rows.

1 LOGO	4	7	10
2 NAVBAR	5	8	11
3 SIDEBAR	6	9	

6 There is a grid-auto-columns property to set the width of columns that are added. As with grid-auto-rows, it enables us to set a width for any new columns that are added, however many there may be. Add this line to the CSS for your grid_container div:

```
grid-auto-columns: 300px;
```

7 Save your web page and open it in your browser. Now, boxes 10 and 11 are 300px wide like the other columns.

1 LOGO	4	7	10
2 NAVBAR	5	8	11
3 SIDEBAR	6	9	

Positioning grid boxes

One of the great things about a grid is that you can control where items sit in it. Their position is not tied to where they are defined in your HTML. You can also set grid boxes to span multiple rows or columns.

 First, let's clean up our CSS and HTML after those experiments. If you have more than nine grid boxes, delete the extras. Set your grid container using these styles. Note that I've explicitly set the size for five rows, and I've removed the grid-auto-columns and grid-auto-rows CSS:

```css
.grid_container{
    display: grid;
    grid-template-columns: repeat(3, 300px);
    grid-template-rows: 100px repeat(4,
        250px);
    grid-gap: 20px;
}
```

 You can change any item's grid row or column using the grid-row and grid-column properties. Columns and rows are numbered from the top left. Try this:

```css
.grid-box-7 {
    grid-column: 2;
    grid-row: 2;
    background-color: yellow;
}
```

 Save your web page and open it in your browser. You'll see that grid box 7 has moved into column 2 and row 2. The other boxes run in their usual pattern around it.

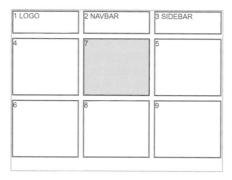

Hot tip

Sidebars are sometimes used for promotional content that would be offputting if it was the main thing the visitor saw when visiting the site. Using this technique with media queries, you can place the sidebar on the left on big screens, but push it to the bottom of a single-column mobile design.

4 A grid item can span multiple columns. Set the start position as before, add a slash, and then set how many columns you want it to span, like this:

```
.grid-box-2 { grid-column: 2 / span 2; }
```

5 When you view your updated web page in your browser, you'll see that box 2 now spans two columns.

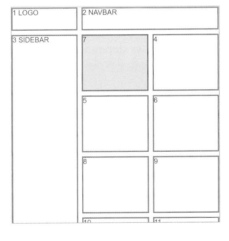

6 There is a different way to express a span. You can use the grid line numbers for the start and the end of the span. The grid lines start at 1 in the top left outside the first box, and are then between the boxes. This is almost the same as what we've been doing so far, except that you need to add 1 to the end of the span. To cover column 3, you need to end at grid line 4. If you use the value of -1, it will span to the final row or column. (The minus means it's counting back from the other side.) Add this to make the sidebar stretch down the screen, alongside all the other boxes:

```
.grid-box-3 { grid-row: 2 / -1; }
```

Hot tip

There are other ways to position elements, too. You can name grid lines and grid areas.

Hot tip

You can use the row-gap and column-gap properties to set the space between the grid items. The gap property sets both at once. Use these properties on the grid container. For example:

gap: 16px;

155

Beware

When you use -1 to set the end of a span, it only counts the explicit grid. Any items that were positioned and sized automatically, including with grid-auto-rows and grid-auto-columns, won't be spanned.

Don't forget

You can use a simple grid to lay out a responsive website without needing to use media queries.

Hot tip

Some people have huge monitors today, so your website might be easier to use if you set a maximum width on your page content. You can use the max-width CSS property, like this:

body
{max-width: 2000px;}

Using auto-fit in the grid

So far, we've been able to create a nicely aligned page layout using CSS, with the flexibility to reposition things in it. Now it gets really exciting, because the auto-fit capability of the grid means that content can flow according to the available space.

1 We don't know how many columns or rows there will be in this grid, because it depends on the size of the browser window. So, let's set grid-box-2 to span until the final column:

```
.grid-box-2 { grid-column: 2 / -1; }
```

2 Now, instead of setting a fixed number of columns, we'll change the number of columns for the grid container to the auto-fit value:

```
grid-template-columns: repeat(auto-fit, 300px);
```

3 View the web page in your browser, and drag the edge of your browser window to make it narrower. The grid reflows depending on the width of the browser window.

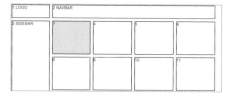

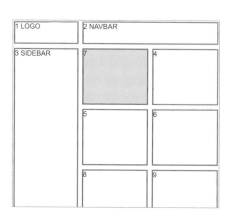

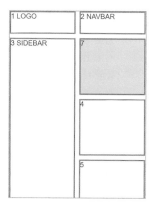

4 So far, the grid boxes are the same width, but there is often empty space on the right of the browser

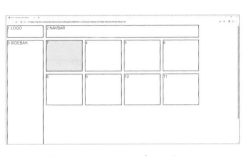

window because there isn't enough room for a box there. We can use the auto-fit function together with the minmax() function to allocate the free space to the content boxes. The minmax() function sets a minimum and maximum size for the columns. We can use the fr unit as a width to say how much of the free space we want each column to have. It works like the flex grow value. By setting the maximum to 1fr, we can make the columns stretch to fill the space available. They share the free space equally. Here is how you use auto-fit with minmax():

```
grid-template-columns: repeat(auto-fit,
                        minmax(300px, 1fr));
```

5 Refresh the file in your browser window and try resizing it. You should see the grid flow to fill the viewport. Boxes will be no smaller than 300px and will stretch to fill the viewport. There is one problem: when the viewport is really narrow, the minimum sizing breaks down. I'll explain that and show you how to fix it next.

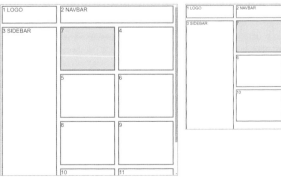

Hot tip

There is a grid shorthand that combines the grid features we've discussed in a single line. It's not easy or intuitive, though, so I recommend sticking with the long form.

157

Hot tip

As well as auto-fit, there is an auto-fill option. The auto-fill option may leave empty columns. See below auto-fill (upper picture) versus auto-fit.

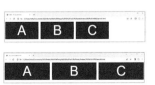

Fixing the final bugs

We now have a responsive grid layout, with boxes that increase in size to use the screen space available. There's a problem, though...

Hot tip

You could use a media query to push box 3 down the screen on a narrow viewport.

1 What happens when the viewport is really narrow? Try it in your browser and you'll see that the minimum width rule doesn't work in column 2.

2 The reason for this is that we're forcing the grid to have two columns with some of our positioning. We have put box 7 in column 2, and we've set column 2 to span columns. These rules are forcing the grid to have a column 2 that there isn't enough room for. To fix it, first find the rules for .grid-box-7 and .grid-box-2 in your CSS.

Hot tip

I set the minimum width at 653px because that's the minimum width to fit two columns. It reflects the width and border of the boxes, the gap between them, and the default body padding of 16px.

3 Now, wrap those rules in the following media query so that they only apply when the browser window is at least 653 pixels wide. Remember: you need to put { and } curly braces around the CSS for .grid-box-7 and .grid-box-2:

```
@media screen and
(min-width: 653px)
{/* Rules for box
2 and 7 here*/ }
```

4 Your web page shows as a single column in a narrow browser window, but box 3 is still really deep. That's because the grid-row property is set to span multiple rows. To fix it, move box 3's CSS between your new media query brackets. Try it in your browser, and it works, as shown here.

Beware

A narrower grid needs more rows. The new rows are part of the implicit grid. You may need to define more rows in grid-template-rows or use grid-auto-rows to size them. Items like our sidebar can only span the explicit grid.

9 JavaScript for interactive pages

JavaScript enables you to make your web pages interactive. You can check that forms have been completed correctly, update the screen with text or photos, and display randomly chosen special offers. In this chapter, you'll learn the basics and discover some handy code you can adapt for your website.

Hot tip

For security reasons, JavaScript is limited to working within the browser. That means that it can't interfere with the website visitor's computer and access the hard disk, for example.

Hot tip

To tell website visitors who don't have JavaScript what they're missing, put a message between <noscript> and </noscript> tags in your HTML. Anything between these tags will only be presented to the user when JavaScript isn't available.

Right: Cameron Adams (**www.themaninblue. com**) created his arcade game Bunny Hunt using JavaScript. Play it at **http://www. themaninblue.com/ experiment/BunnyHunt/**

What is JavaScript?

While HTML is used to describe the structure of your content, and CSS lets you describe its appearance, JavaScript gives you the power to make the computer perform actions. It is a programming language that you can use to make your web page interactive.

You can, for example:

● Update the screen contents after the page has downloaded.

● Make it easier for visitors to use forms by checking for any errors before the form information is sent to the server.

● Hide or reveal web page content. You might, for example, have different tabbed sections of content, which the user can display on the current web page by clicking on a tab.

● Respond to user actions, including clicks on the page.

JavaScript is widely supported, but users of assistive devices might not be able to use it. Search engines can also struggle with it. For that reason, you should avoid using it for navigation and should ensure that your website still functions well with JavaScript disabled. Take particular care that appropriate alternative content is provided if JavaScript is used to convey information or content.

You also need to take care with updates to parts of the screen that the user might not be looking at. People using screen magnifiers can only see a small part of the screen at a time, but even people using normal browsers can have problems if you update the top of the page with something important after it's scrolled out of view.

How to add JavaScript

Like HTML and CSS, you can write JavaScript using any text editor. I use VS Code (see Chapter 10). There are two ways to add JavaScript to your web page.

 Put your JavaScript between HTML <script> tags, like this:

```
<script>
        alert("Hello!");
</script>
```

Put this code in the body of your HTML document. If you add that example to your web page, you'll  see an alert box that displays "Hello!" when you open the page. You have to click OK to make it go away. The line alert("Hello!"); is the JavaScript that makes that box appear. The <script> tags are the HTML used to add JavaScript to your page.

Alternatively, add an external file. You can put your JavaScript commands into a separate text file and give it a .js extension, and then use a <script> tag to add it into a web page. That means you can share the same JavaScript code across different web pages, or even across different websites. Your website will load more quickly if you add your external JavaScript file at the bottom of your HTML file, just before the closing </body> tag. Here's the code to add an external JavaScript file called alertbox.js:

```
<script src="alertbox.js"></script>
```

Your alertbox.js file could be just one line:

```
alert("Hello!");
```

You can add a JavaScript file from somebody else's server, like this:

```
<script src="http://www.example.com/alertbox.js">
</script>
```

Services like Google Analytics will provide some code for you to paste into your web page that looks a bit like this.

The double quote marks are also called speech marks. They are a single symbol on your keyboard. Don't type two apostrophes instead.

If you use an external JavaScript file, you don't include <script> tags in it. In this chapter, I'll assume you're putting your JavaScript in your HTML document.

If your JavaScript needs to run before the page is displayed, you need to put it in the head of your HTML document.

Creating functions

Web designers often create functions, which are groups of JavaScript commands that should be executed (or carried out) in sequence. All these commands can then be executed by just telling the browser the name of the function to use, and when to use it. There are several benefits to using functions:

- It makes it easier to reuse JavaScript on a web page. You can run the same function in different circumstances, and could even do slightly different things with the function each time. You could use the same reveal function to reveal two different boxes, for example.

- Functions enable you to control when commands are executed. If your JavaScript is outside a function, the browser will try to run it as soon as possible. Most of the time, you'll want to use JavaScript to respond to something that's happening on the web page, so being able to defer JavaScript actions until the right time is extremely valuable.

- Functions make it easier to understand what your JavaScript code does so that you can maintain and adapt it more easily.

Here's an example of a function that displays two alert messages. I've given the function the name "welcome". Because of the way the alert command works, the visitor has to click the OK button to get each alert box to go away. Alert boxes are good for testing and learning, but they're irritating for users, so I don't recommend using them on real web pages:

```
function welcome()
    {
        alert("Hello!");
        alert("Thanks for visiting my site!");
    }
```

A function has two ordinary brackets at the end of its name, and curly braces are used to mark the start and end of that function. You can put this JavaScript code (from the word "function" down to the closing curly bracket) where you previously put the single alert command. When you reload your web page, you won't see anything happen, because we haven't told JavaScript to run this function yet.

You can see how the alert command works more clearly now: the bit between the double quotes is what appears in the alert box.

Responding to user actions

Now we have created our JavaScript function called welcome(), we need a way to trigger it. JavaScript is event-driven. That means JavaScript commands are usually triggered when something happens, such as somebody clicking a link or moving the mouse over an image. We need to add an event listener to the page, which will start an action when a particular event occurs.

1 JavaScript can detect clicks on any element, such as a picture or a paragraph. We'll start by using a

button, and we'll give it the ID of "welcome_button". Create an HTML document that includes these lines:

```
<form>
      <input type="button" id="welcome_button"
             value="Greet me!">
</form>
```

2 Now, we'll add the code that listens out for clicks on that button. It uses getElementById to find the button in the web page using the ID we gave it. We create a variable (a name) for it, which is the_button. We then add an event listener to the_button, which starts our welcome function when the_button is clicked. I'll show you all the JavaScript, including the welcome() function you've already seen, to help you see where everything goes:

```
<script>
function welcome()
{
      alert("Hello!");
      alert("Thanks for visiting my site!");
}

var the_button = document.
      getElementById("welcome_button");
the_button.addEventListener("click", welcome);

</script>
```

3 Load the page in your browser. Click the button to see the welcome() function run, displaying two alert boxes.

With JavaScript, you need to get the capital letters in the right place. Pay close attention to getElementById and addEventListener.

If you only want the function to run the first time the button is clicked, add this inside the function:

the_button.removeEvent Listener("click", welcome);

JavaScript outside a function runs straight away, including the instruction to add the event listener here.

Changing styles

You can use JavaScript to change the style of elements on the page. It's a bit like applying CSS code from JavaScript, although the way the properties are written is different.

 For this example, create a simple web page with a <h1> heading, a paragraph and an image. Give the <img> tag an ID of "photo" and the paragraph a class of "bodytext". I've floated the image on the right and given it a margin:

```
<body style="background-color: antiquewhite;">
<img id="photo" src="images/london1.jpg"
style="float: right; margin-left: 16px;">
<h1>Let's experiment with JavaScript!</h1>
<p class="bodytext">Lorem ipsum dolor sit amet,
consectetuer adipiscing elit.</p>
</body>
```

Add this JavaScript to your web page:

```
<script>
var my_picture = document.
    getElementById("photo");
my_picture.style.border="16px darkgoldenrod
    double";
</script>
```

Refresh the web page in your browser, and you'll see that the JavaScript has given the image a darkgoldenrod-colored double border.

4 In Chapter 7, you learned how to use CSS selectors to target style rules at different parts of the page. You can also use them to select page elements in JavaScript using querySelector(). This code finds the <h1> tag and restyles its font and color. It goes between your <script> tags:

```
var my_heading = document.querySelector("h1");
my_heading.style.fontFamily = "arial";
my_heading.style.color = "saddlebrown";
```

5 You can also use querySelector() to match other CSS selectors, including class names. Here, we'll match the paragraph with the class name "bodytext" and change the font, color, background color, fontsize, padding and box shadow properties:

```
var my_paragraph = document.querySelector(
      ".bodytext");
my_paragraph.style.color = "white";
my_paragraph.style.backgroundColor = "maroon";
my_paragraph.style.fontSize = "32px";
my_paragraph.style.padding = "16px";
my_paragraph.style.boxShadow =
      "sienna 8px 8px 2px";
```

6 You can also use JavaScript to change the text content:

```
my_paragraph.textContent = "London is the most
      wonderful city to visit."
```

Hot tip

I've used the variable names my_heading, my_picture, my_paragraph and all_h2s. You could choose different variable names if you prefer.

165

Hot tip

JavaScript variable names cannot include spaces or words JavaScript uses for its language. Names are case-sensitive, so my_picture and my_Picture are two different variables.

Let's experiment with JavaScript!

London is the most wonderful city to visit.

...cont'd

7 You can only use querySelector() to select the first matching item on the page. If you have multiple items you want to style, you need to use querySelectorAll(). It gives you all of the items in a group, and then you use something called a loop to style each one of them in turn. Add some <h2> tags to your HTML, perhaps with some paragraphs between them to space them out, and then add this between your <script> tags to style them:

```
var all_h2s = document.querySelectorAll("h2");
for (let i=0; i<all_h2s.length; i++)
{
all_h2s[i].style.backgroundColor = "firebrick";
all_h2s[i].style.color = "white";
}
```

Hot tip

The for instruction tells the browser we want to repeat the instructions in the curly braces {} after it. In the rounded brackets (), we say how many times we'll repeat. We'll set up a counter called i, and start it at 0. We say we'll keep going as long as our counter is less than the number of items in our all_h2s list. Each time we finish working with one of the list items, we tell the browser to increase the counter by 1. (i++ is a short way to say add 1 to i.)

8 Open your updated web page in your browser, and you will see that the <h2> tags are now styled too. Try experimenting by selecting different parts of the page and styling them in different ways. What we're doing here we could more easily do with CSS, but this technique becomes powerful when we combine styling with events.

Properties you can style

There is a huge number of properties you can style using JavaScript. Here are some of the more useful ones. They could be used to change parts of a user interface to give your user feedback or provide additional information. Use them like this:

```
element.style.propertyName = "new value"
```

- background, backgroundColor
- border, borderColor, BorderLeft (and other sides)
- boxShadow
- display
- font, fontFamily, fontSize, fontStyle, fontWeight
- height, width
- left, top, right, bottom: for the position of an element
- margin, marginLeft (and other sides)
- opacity, visibility
- overflow, overflowX, overflowY
- padding, paddingBottom (and other sides)
- position (for example, absolute or relative)
- textDecoration, textDecorationColor, textDecorationLine, textDecorationStyle
- textShadow
- z-index

Beware

You must match the capital letters exactly. Luckily, the pattern is clear: they all start with a lowercase letter and use an uppercase letter for the start of each new word in the property. Unlike CSS, no hyphens are used here.

Changing an element's content
You can also change the following properties of an element where they apply. You don't need to put style in front of these:

```
my_picture.src = "images/london2.jpg"
```

- textContent, for changing the text in an element
- innerHTML, for changing the HTML code in an element
- src, for changing the source file of an image

Detecting other events

The table below shows other events you can listen for on an element. This code uses box shadow to add a glow around a button when the mouse is over it.

Above: The button glows when the mouse rolls over it.

1 Let's reuse our button HTML:

```
<form><input type="button" id="welcome_button"
             value="Greet me!"></form>
```

2 Add this JavaScript between <script> tags, before your </body> tag. We're adding two events, mouseover and mouseout, and we're using them to trigger different functions. The box shadow adds a glowing halo effect:

```
var the_button = document.getElementById
      ("welcome_button");
the_button.addEventListener
      ("mouseover", glow_on);
the_button.addEventListener
      ("mouseout", glow_off);

function glow_on(){
      the_button.style.boxShadow =
            "lime 0px 0px 32px";}

function glow_off() {
      the_button.style.boxShadow = "none";}
```

You can achieve a similar effect to this by using the :hover and :focus pseudo styles in CSS, which is simpler.

You can use a timer to trigger an action. Use the setTimeout() command and give it the JavaScript to execute later, with the length of delay in milliseconds. For example: setTimeout("welcome();", 1250);

Event name	What triggers it
mouseover	The mouse pointer is over something.
mouseout	The mouse pointer rolls away again.
click	Something is clicked.
focus	The user enters a form field or uses the keyboard to select a link.
blur	The user moves away from a form field or a link selected by keyboard.
change	The user changes a form field, such as choosing a radio button, and then moves their focus away from that field.
load	The web page loads (see page 169).
unload	The user goes to a different page.

Showing and hiding content

One of the most useful things you can do with JavaScript is to show or hide content on the page so that the page can be updated or users can control what they see.

1 To tell the browser which content you would like to hide or reveal, wrap it in <div> and </div> tags and give it an ID in the opening tag, like this:

```
<div id="hidden_box">Optional box</div>
```

2 Add a control to show the content when you want to. For example, add a button and give it an ID of show_terms:

```
<form>
<input type="button" id="show_terms"
value="Show terms">
</form>
```

3 Add this JavaScript before the </body> tag:

```
<script>
show_button = document.getElementById
      ("show_terms");
show_button.addEventListener
      ("click", display_box);
hidden_box = document.getElementById
      ("hidden_box");

function hide_box()
      { hidden_box.style.display = "none"; }
function display_box()
      { hidden_box.style.display = "block"; }
</script>
```

4 Change your <body> tag so that the section is hidden when the page loads using JavaScript. This ensures that those who do not have JavaScript can still see the content, but that the content is hidden from those with JavaScript when the page loads:

```
<body onload="hide_box();">
```

5 Test it works as expected in your browser. When you design something like this, make sure it's obvious to users that they can click to reveal new content; otherwise, they might not realize they're missing anything.

Hot tip

I'm using the onload event here to add JavaScript to my HTML <body> tag. In a similar way, you can use onmouseover, onmouseout, onclick, onfocus, onblur and onchange to add JavaScript code to tags including paragraphs, links and form fields.

Hot tip

Using an <a> tag with an onclick event makes it easy for people to see where they should click, because the clickable area will look like other links on the page. You need to disable the link destination, though. To do that, use href="javascript:;" It needs both a colon and a semicolon before the closing double quotes.

Customizing by date/time

JavaScript can make simple decisions about which instructions it should run. In plain English, the code looks like this:

```
if (test to be done)
      {instructions to carry out if that
            condition is satisfied}
else
      {instructions to carry out if
            that condition is not satisfied}
```

You don't always need the else section. In a form validation, for example, you want to display an error message if the user makes a mistake, but do nothing otherwise.

Using JavaScript, the web page can see what the date and time are on the user's computer, so it can display special messages depending on the time of day, day of the week, or the month. It's a nice way to personalize the experience, and a great way to experiment with JavaScript if statements!

Don't forget

You need to put your JavaScript functions between <script> tags or in an external JavaScript file. If you get confused, download the sample code from my website.

Getting date and time information

Here's some code that will work out the date, month, day of the week and hour:

```
function the_date()
{today=new Date();temp=today.getDate();return temp;}

function the_month()
{today=new Date();temp=today.getMonth();return temp;}

function the_day()
{today=new Date();temp=today.getDay();return temp;}

function the_hour()
{today=new Date();temp=today.getHours();return temp;}
```

When you use these functions, they will give you these numbers:

Function	Number returned
the_date()	Returns today's date (1-31).
the_month()	Returns the month number, where 0 is January and 11 is December.
the_day()	Returns the day of the week, where 0 is Sunday, 1 is Monday, 2 is Tuesday, up to 6 for Saturday.
the_hour()	Returns the hour from the time now (24-hour clock).

Displaying timely messages

Let's display a message depending on the time of day.

1 In your HTML, create an empty div that the JavaScript can insert your message into. You can add a background color and text styling to this if you like. This empty box won't appear on the web page until your JavaScript adds content to it:

```
<div id="greetings_box"></div>
```

2 Add the functions on the facing page, inside <script> and </script> tags, before your </body> tag.

3 Now, add the following code, also between the <script> tags. It sets up a message with some default text and uses our function called the_hour(). It replaces the text in the message variable, depending on how late it is:

```
var message="Hello";
if (the_hour()<12)
        {message = "Good morning!"; }
else if (the_hour()<18)
        {message = "Good afternoon!";}
else
        {message = "Good evening!";}
```

4 Finally, add these lines of JavaScript to output the message. We're using the textContent property to do this. If we wanted to include HTML formatting in our message, we'd use innerHTML instead:

```
var output_box=document.getElementById
        ("greetings_box");
output_box.textContent=message;
```

This works because of the order the tests are in. It checks whether the hour is less than 12, and only then does it check whether it's less than 18. To get to that point, we know it's more than 12, so we can confidently show a "Good afternoon!" message. If the hour is later than 18, it shows a "Good evening!" message. If you jumble those tests up, it won't work.

...cont'd

Adding multiple tests

What if you want to test for something that can't be arranged so elegantly, such as working out whether it's the weekend or not?

You can add multiple tests inside the rounded brackets of the if statement. If you want an action to be taken when either of the conditions is true, you use || to combine them, like this:

```
if (the_day()==6 || the_day()==0)
        { output_box.textContent+=
                " It's the weekend!"; }
```

This message will be added to any other messages in the output_box div. That's because I used += instead of = when updating its textContent property. The += operator adds on to the end of what's already there. I started the new text with a space, otherwise it would be tight against any text already there.

If you only want an action to be taken when both the conditions are true, you use && to combine them, in place of ||.

Here's some code to display a message only if the date is the 14th and the month is February. Remember that months are numbered starting at zero, so February is month number 1:

```
if (the_date()==14 && the_month()==1)
        { output_box.textContent+=
                " Happy Valentine's Day!"; }
```

Beware

Don't mix up your brackets! The if command uses rounded brackets around the things it's basing a decision on (such as whether the date is the 14th and the month February). The command then uses curly braces around the commands it will execute if those conditions are satisfied. Every opening bracket needs a closing bracket of the same type.

You could add messages for a number of holidays that your customers celebrate so that your website always appears up to date. You could display a Christmas message for all of December by simply checking whether the month is 11.

JavaScript comparison operators

The table below shows all the comparisons you can make:

==	Equal to
!=	Not equal to
>	Greater than
<	Less than
>=	Greater than or equal to
<=	Less than or equal to

Advanced form validation

As you saw in Chapter 6, browsers have some basic form validation built in today. However, with JavaScript you can do more specific tests. You can validate:

- The length of information entered – for example, if the length is too short for the password rules.

- Whether something has been typed in that exactly matches what you're looking for.

- Whether a particular symbol or word has been entered as part of the information entered. For example, does an email address include an @ sign and a full stop, which is required for the domain name? Chrome only checks for an @ sign.

- Whether a particular checkbox has been selected.

Friendly form validation

There are two ways you can validate your form. You can provide feedback as people are completing the form. You could, for example, check an email address as soon as it's been typed in and then show an immediate warning message if it's invalid. The advantage of this is that you can offer feedback where and when it's needed most. Alternatively, you can offer feedback when the whole form has been completed and the **Submit** button has been pressed, perhaps highlighting any problem fields in red. The advantage of this is that users can have one passthrough entering information and a second passthrough fixing any problems, which might make the process seem quicker.

Two important guidelines will ensure that your validation is seen as helpful, not hectoring:

1. **Publish the rules up-front.** If a password has to be at least eight characters, tell people before you ask them to make one up. You'll only annoy them if you tell them for the first time after they've typed it in.

2. **Don't over-validate.** Telling people their name or phone number is too long, or that their address is wrong, is annoying when they're right. Take particular care to ensure that long names and foreign addresses and phone numbers can be entered into your forms without triggering warnings.

You can find more advanced form validation scripts online, which will (for example) test that the @ sign and full stop are in the right places in the email address. Search the web for "form validation JavaScript".

173

Test your forms give the right messages by trying different inputs that match and don't match what you're looking for.

Checking password length

Using JavaScript, we can check that a password is at least eight characters when the user is choosing it.

You could use onchange to start the JavaScript, but the field starts off empty. If it's not changed, it would remain empty but the validation routine wouldn't run.

1 First, let's set up our form field. I've left out all the other form elements and just given you the essentials here. There's an empty div where we will warn the user their password is too short, if it is:

```html
<form>
<label for="password">Enter New Password:
</label>
<input type="password"
       id="password_box" name="password"
       onblur="validate_password();">
<div id="password_warning"></div>
</form>
```

2 Now, add your validate_password() function. It looks up the password_box ID, gets the form field's value, and checks whether its length is less than 8 characters:

```html
<script>
function validate_password()
{
if (document.getElementById('password_box').
value.length<8) {
        var warning_box = document.
            getElementById('password_warning');
            warning_box.innerHTML =
            "<b>Password must be at least 8
            characters.</b>";
        var pw_field = document.getElementById
            ('password_box');
        pw_field.style.border= "2px red solid";
                        }
}
</script>
```

You can use the "required" attribute on a form field to stop the form being submitted without the field being completed.

3 Try it! Enter something in the password box and then tab or click off of it. If you enter fewer than eight characters, the validate_password() routine changes the HTML in your password_warning div to some warning text.

Each form element needs to have a unique ID. Otherwise, your JavaScript might end up testing the wrong parts of the form.

Enter New Password: ••
Password must be at least 8 characters.

Checking text in forms

To check whether somebody has entered a particular word or name into a textbox, use this snippet of JavaScript.

1 First, let's set up our form field:

```
<form>
<label for="first_name">Enter First Name:
</label>
<input type="text" id="first_name"
       name="password" onblur="check_name();">
</form>
```

2 Let's add the JavaScript now to check the name when it's entered. We could do a simple check for a name, like this:

```
if (document.getElementById("first_name").
value=="Karen")
```

That won't catch the name if there's a space before or after it, or if there's no capital "K", so here's an alternative:

```
<script>
function check_name() {
       if (document.getElementById("first_name").
       value.toLowerCase().indexOf("karen")!=-1)
              { alert("Hello Karen!"); }
}
</script>
```

3 Try entering different names into the first name box. Only Karen triggers a friendly greeting.

The toLowerCase() part of the code converts the text entered to lowercase before it is tested. The message appears whether you type in "Karen", "KAREN", or any other variant. If you enter a space first, it still works because it shows a message if Karen is any part of the text entered. Take care with this. If you check for Leo using indexOf(), it would match Leon and Leonard too.

Form test

This page says

Hello Karen!

First Name: KaReN

OK

Hot tip

Make sure you test for a match with the lowercase version of the word or name (between the rounded brackets of the if statement). Otherwise, this function will never trigger a message.

Don't forget

You can sometimes use a select menu to restrict what people can enter. Then, you can look for an exact match.

175

Hot tip

indexOf() gives the number -1 if the text you're looking for isn't there. Otherwise, it gives a number that shows where it is in the form field, starting at zero for the first character.

Checkboxes and numbers

Has a checkbox been checked?

You can test whether a checkbox has been checked, too, so that you can hide or reveal different parts of the form accordingly. Assuming you have a checkbox with an ID of options, this is how you test whether it's been selected:

```
if (document.getElementById("options").checked==true)
{ code to show/hide options goes here }
```

You can use the same code to test whether a radio button with an ID of options has been selected. It feels more intuitive for content to appear or disappear when a box is checked than when a radio button is selected, though.

Checking numbers in forms

You can combine what you have learned about form validation with the number comparisons you saw earlier to test numbers entered into forms. Add an input box in your HTML form:

```
<label for="age">Age:</label>
<input type="text" id="age">
<input type="button" onclick="validate();"
       value="Check">
```

You can then use JavaScript to display suitable promotions to children when the button is clicked:

```
<script>
function validate()
{
if (document.getElementById("age").value<18)
       {alert("Promotion for under 18s");}
}
</script>
```

We're using alert boxes here because they're simple for testing. In a real website, you would change the on-page content instead.

Right: On my website, visitors can use a simple form to chat to a virtual version of me. It uses JavaScript to check for certain keywords in the text entered, so it can often appear to give an intelligent response. You can find it and my other JavaScript games at http://www.sean.co.uk/a/javascriptgames/index.shtm

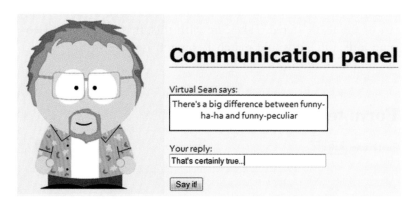

176

Adding random content

You can make your website feel more dynamic by adding some randomly chosen content to it. This could be used to share a random tip or joke, or call attention to random special offers.

To do this, you need to store a list of content in an array. An array is a set of variables that all have the same name. To tell the individual items apart, they are numbered starting at zero. The variable name has square brackets after it with the number between them – for example: item[0], item[1], item[2], etc.

1 In your web page, add an empty div section with the ID of tip:

```
<div id="tip"></div>
```

2 Add this JavaScript code to your page. It puts a list of tips into an array, picks one at random and inserts it into the "tip" div. The Math.random() function gives us a number between 0 and 1, so we multiply it (using the * symbol) by the number of tips we have. We then use Math.floor to round down, to give us a tip number. The code includes an event listener to start the tip_setup() function when the page loads. This is an alternative to adding the onload attribute to the HTML <body> tag. This way, you can keep your JavaScript wholly separated from your HTML:

```
<script>
window.addEventListener("load", tip_setup);
function tip_setup()
{
tips=new Array();
tips[0]="First tip goes here";
tips[1]="Second tip here";
tips[2]="Third tip here";
var chosen_one=Math.floor(Math.random()
      * tips.length);
document.getElementById('tip')
      .innerHTML=tips[chosen_one];
}
</script>
```

3 Increase the tip number by 1 for each tip you add:

```
tips[3]="Extra tip here";
```

Above: I used some JavaScript similar to this to create a random Writing Wisdom box on my website.

Hot tip

Each tip should have a unique number, and no numbers should be skipped. The code will always pick randomly from all the tips you've provided.

Don't forget

You can use links or any other HTML in your tips. Use CSS to style the content of your #tip box as you would normally.

177

Next steps with JavaScript

JavaScript is considerably more complex than HTML and CSS, so I can only introduce you to the basics here and give you some example code you can cut, paste and edit to your requirements. This chapter gives you enough knowledge to experiment with scripts you find online, and to start making your own simple effects for your web pages.

One way you can save time in writing your JavaScript, and ensure that it works well across a wide range of browsers, is to use a JavaScript library or framework. This is a collection of often-used JavaScript functions. Using one means that you can focus on designing your site, instead of reinventing the wheel by creating something like a new show/hide routine, a problem that many thousands of developers have already solved before you.

Popular frameworks include:

- **React**, which was developed by social networking company Meta and is used to make web interfaces.

- **Node.js**, which can run on the server to generate web pages that are then sent to the user's browser. This is a different use of JavaScript from what we've covered here. One reason Node.js is popular is that it enables developers to use the same language (JavaScript) in both the browser (the front end) and the server (the back end).

- **jQuery**, which makes it easy to create the kinds of visual effects often associated with social networking websites, such as boxes that scroll into view or page elements that fade in and out. jQuery also simplifies a lot of the basic JavaScript and CSS activities you might want to undertake, such as adding content to a page or removing it again.

Do you need to learn JavaScript? Not necessarily. JavaScript is an important foundation for websites that require updating in real time, or that need to wow their visitors with interactive effects. But many websites can work without it.

If you do learn how to create JavaScript, though, you'll soon spot opportunities to use it to make your website more interactive, useful and fun. Once you've mastered HTML and CSS, JavaScript is the next logical step in building your website and your web design skills.

Beware

Older browsers might not support some JavaScript and CSS features in the same way, or at all. For example, animation isn't supported on some older browsers. However, they only account for about 1% of the web population today, according to caniuse.com

10 Tools for website design

Using the right tools can save you a lot of time when you design your website.

Editing in VS Code

Visual Studio Code (VS Code) is a free text-editing tool from Microsoft. It has features for writing and editing code in a number of computer languages, including HTML, CSS and JavaScript. It's available for Windows, Mac and Linux computers.

1 Visit **https://code.visualstudio.com/** in your browser to download the software and install it.

2 Start Visual Studio Code.

3 From the **File** menu, choose **New Text File**.

4 Your untitled text file opens with an option to select a language. Click it.

```
≡ Untitled-1  ✕

   1    Select a language, or open a different editor to get started.
        Start typing to dismiss or don't show this again.
```

180

5 Choose HTML, CSS or JavaScript from the menu.

```
Select Language Mode

Auto Detect
 ▓ Batch (bat)                                      languages (identifier)
 ≡ BibTeX (bibtex)
 ≡ Binary (code-text-binary)
 C  C (c)
 C⁺ C# (csharp)
 G⁺ C++ (cpp)
 ◎ Clojure (clojure)
 ⚙ CoffeeScript (coffeescript)
 ⬢ Compose (dockercompose)
 #  CSS (css)
 G⁺ CUDA C++ (cuda-cpp)
 ◖ Dart (dart)
 ≡ Diff (diff)
 ⬢ Docker (dockerfile)
 ◇ F# (fsharp)
 ◆ Git Commit Message (git-commit)
 ≡ Git Rebase Message (git-rebase)
```

6 The editor helps you to complete your code. When you start to type an HTML tag, for example, the editor opens a menu showing possible options. Use the arrow keys to move up and down the menu. Click an option to choose it, or press the **Tab** key.

```
1   <!DOCTYPE html>
2   <html lang="en">
3   <head>
4       <meta charset="utf-8">
5       <title>Web Design in Easy Steps</title>
6   </head>
7   <bo
        body
        bdo
        blockquote
        button
```

The editor understands the symmetry of your code. When you type a quote mark, the editor automatically adds a closing one for you. When you type a curly bracket in your CSS code, the editor adds a closing one. It's a great time saver, but it can introduce errors if you don't notice!

7 The editor colors the different parts of your code so that it's easier to read. In CSS, for example, selectors are dark red, properties are bright red, and values are blue or green. When you include a color, a tiny box of that color appears next to it in your code.

```
1   body {
2       background-color: aquamarine;
3       color: #7f888f;
4       font-family: sans-serif;
5   }
```

VS Code enables you to add extensions to help with tasks like validating and formatting your code. Click the **Extensions** button on the Activity Bar on the left to install and manage extensions. Try W3C Web Validator for checking your HTML.

8 If you're working with a big file, the minimap on the right helps you to navigate it. It's a tiny snapshot of your code, including the color coding. Click and drag in the minimap to quickly jump to the part of the file you need to edit. This is handy when editing very large files.

9 VS Code automatically indents your code when you open a block-level tag, such as <body>, <div> or <p>. This makes it easier to see your document structure.

Adding folders in VS Code

Adding folders makes it easier to browse and manage all the files that make up your website.

1 Click the **Explorer** button in the Activity Bar on the left.

2 In the Explorer pane, click **Open Folder**. Browse to your website folder, select it and click **Add**.

3 You can now use the Explorer pane to easily find and edit files. When you hover over it, buttons appear at the top to create a new file or a new folder, to refresh the pane (useful if you add or remove files outside of VS Code), and to collapse all the folders so that you can see an overview of the site more easily. Click the arrow beside a folder name to expand that folder. Click a filename to open it.

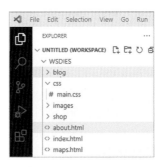

4 Click the **Search** option on the Activity Bar on the left. You can now search, and even replace text, across all the files in your website.

Testing your site in VS Code

Connect VS Code to your browser so that you can easily test the web pages you're working on.

1 On the Activity Bar on the left, click the **Run and Debug** icon to open the appropriate pane.

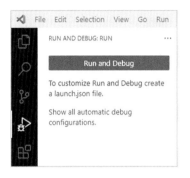

2 When the pane opens, click the big blue **Run and Debug** button.

Don't forget

Your file is saved when you run the debugger to view it in your browser. If you're making experimental changes, keep a clean copy of the file somewhere safe.

3 Choose which browser you want to use. Your file will be saved and it will open in your web browser.

4 You can ignore the variables, watch and call stack panes in the debugger. They're not useful for HTML and CSS, although they can help with advanced JavaScript projects.

5 When you've made edits and want to refresh the web page in your browser, click the **Restart** button on the **Run and Debug** toolbar. This looks like a green circular arrow. The toolbar appears at the top of your window, but you can click on the left of it and drag it somewhere else.

Hot tip

To stop the debugger and hide the Run and Debug toolbar, click the **Stop** button on it. This looks like a red box.

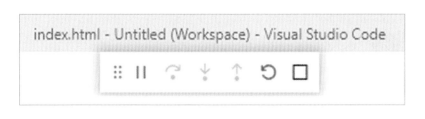

183

Using Chrome DevTools

There's a powerful set of tools built in to the Google Chrome browser. You can use the tools to fix and prototype designs, and study the CSS styles on public websites.

1 In the Chrome browser, right-click something on the page you're interested in. Choose **Inspect** from the menu.

2 The DevTools panels open. The Elements pane (top right) shows the HTML for the element you right-clicked. The Styles pane underneath shows the CSS styles that apply to it. If a style is crossed out, it means another one has overridden it.

You can also edit the HTML in the Elements pane, which can help with testing your CSS.

3 You can edit the CSS. At the top of the Styles pane is an element.style selector. Add new styles here and you can see them applied to your chosen element on the web page.

4 To copy the styles on an element, including any you added in DevTools, right-click the element in the Elements pane, and choose **Copy Styles**. You can then paste these into your editing tool.

It doesn't matter whether the web page you're inspecting is on the web or stored on your computer.

5 Click the first button on the left above the Elements pane. It enables you to select any element on the page.

6 When you hover over the page, a pop-up box gives you information about the element under your cursor. You can instantly see – for example – the colors, margin and padding. Click an element to select it and update the Styles pane.

DevTools gives you a quick and safe way to do web design experiments, but your work is not saved. Make sure you copy the code from DevTools and paste it into your HTML or CSS editing tool.

7 To see the final styles that were applied to the element, missing out any that were overridden, click the **Computed** tab in the lower panel. It looks like the image below.

8 Click the **Group** checkbox to organize the text, layout and appearance styles. This makes it much easier to see how the style instructions work together on the page.

9 Click the arrow on a style in the Computed tab to go to it on the Styles tab. This shows you where it is defined in the style sheet and can help you to fix CSS errors.

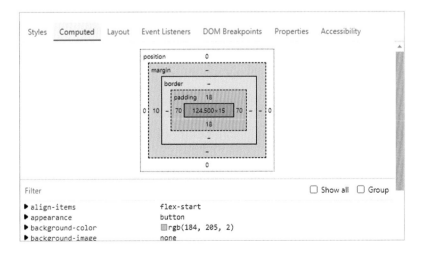

If your content is in a Word document, you can use Word to create a basic web page. Click the File tab and click **Save As**. Change the file type to **Web Page, Filtered**. The HTML is pretty ugly, and it doesn't work for layouts like tables and boxes, but it can save you time marking up each heading and paragraph.

Device testing in DevTools

DevTools helps you to simulate a range of devices so that you can see what your website looks like on them.

1 Click the second button on the left above the Elements pane, which shows a phone and a tablet.

2 The web page is shown as it would appear on a device with a width of 400 pixels. Drag the bar on the right of the web page to extend the viewport.

3 Use the menu to choose a particular device to simulate, or enter custom width and height dimensions. You can zoom in to more clearly see what your page looks like on a device.

11 Content management systems

A content management system (CMS) makes it easier to create and manage sites with lots of content or contributors.

What is a CMS?

A content management system (CMS) enables people to create, edit, publish and manage the content on a website, without needing technical knowledge. It helps in several ways:

- Writers can focus on writing, without having to worry about HTML or any of the technical aspects of adding content to the website. They can style the content using a simple interface that looks and feels similar to a word processor.

- The CMS can automatically add navigation to new content. For example, if you post a new story, the CMS can add links from your homepage and to related articles.

- You can upload images and other content using a simple web-based interface.

- You can update the site more quickly. All you need to do is write the new content in a web form (or paste it in), and press the **Publish** button. You don't have to design HTML files or upload them to the server yourself.

- You can easily edit the site from anywhere. You access your CMS over the web, so you can use it from anywhere in the world where you can get a web connection.

- The CMS enforces consistency in the design, because pages (typically) use the same template. You can easily make site-wide changes to your design by changing the template.

- A CMS will often include the ability to accept comments from site visitors, and give you tools to moderate them.

- You can usually enable different people to have access to the system, with different permissions. Some people might be allowed to edit and delete others' content, for example, while more junior team members can only add their own stories.

You can use a CMS to build your whole website, or could use it just to manage parts of it, such as the news section or the blog.

A CMS might not be appropriate for highly visual sites, or sites with a lot of variation in content or design between different pages or sections. Content management systems most help sites with a lot of textual content that use a standardized design across the site.

Hot tip

Popular content management systems include Drupal (www.drupal.org) and Joomla (www.joomla.org).

188

What is WordPress?

Blogs use a simple content management system. They enable anyone to publish content, which is organized by date. Each article is called a blog post. Supplementary navigation can sort posts into different categories, but the underlying principle is that the content is sorted by date, like an online diary or news feed.

WordPress is a blogging platform, but many people use its sophisticated customization options to build complete websites. As well as adding blog posts, you can add pages that go onto your navbar. You can organize a hierarchy of pages, too, so you can create subsections of pages inside a main section.

There are two different versions of WordPress:

1 **WordPress.com.** This is a service that WordPress will host for you. Setting up a basic site is free, and includes a Secure Sockets Layer (SSL) certificate for secure hosting, 1GB of storage, and dozens of free themes (or layouts) to choose from. Some of the themes are shown below. You'll need to pay to edit your CSS, remove adverts and add analytics. You get a free yoursite.wordpress.com address but I recommend you upgrade to get a real domain name. There are three tiered paid packages to choose from.

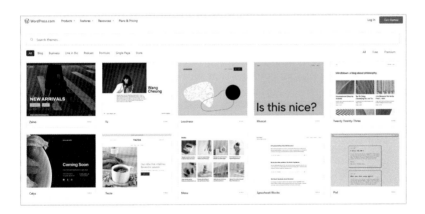

2 **WordPress.org.** This offers PHP software that you need to install on your server. There are over 5,000 themes available, and you have full access to customize them. This is the approach I'd recommend if you want to have complete control over your website design.

You can use a blog to publish news stories, regular opinion columns, a photo a day or pretty much anything else.

Alternative blogging systems include Movable Type (www.movabletype.com) and Blogger (www.blogger.com), which is owned by Google.

Setting up WordPress

I'll show you how you can work with WordPress.org, although there are a lot of similarities between the two versions. Everything on these first two pages applies to WordPress.org only, though.

1 Install WordPress. Many hosting companies offer WordPress hosting, with the installation done for you. If you want to use WordPress, the easiest solution is to choose one of these hosting companies. Mine walked me through the installation process, prompting me to choose a theme and any plug-in features I'd like to add.

2 Log in. When WordPress has been set up, you should see a default template when you visit your website. It might differ from mine.

3 On your Dashboard, click **Appearance** on the left. Click **Add New Theme** to browse the catalog of themes. You can search using a keyword (e.g. "music"), and use the Feature Filter to choose the subject of your blog, the features it includes and the type of layout it uses. Imagine what the theme would look like with your own content in it, especially your own pictures. I recommend you focus on responsive themes that work well on all devices.

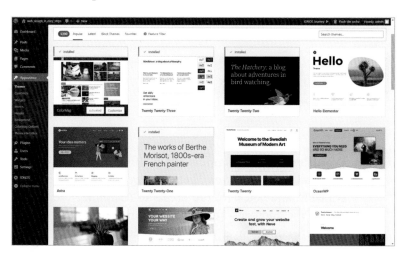

Hot tip

When you're logged in to WordPress, you'll see your blog title in the top left of the screen. You can click it to visit your public-facing website.

Hot tip

To change your website's title and/or tagline, log in to WordPress and click **Settings**.

4 Click a theme to preview it. When you've found one you like, click to install it. This adds it to your WordPress CMS, but it doesn't change your website's appearance. To start using a theme, click **Appearance** on the left. You can see all your installed themes, including small pictures of them. Activate one to start using it on your live website.

Beware

The page templates in WordPress are coded using PHP. It's best to learn the basics of PHP syntax before making significant changes, to ensure you don't introduce bugs. But, if you're adept at HTML, you should be able to make minor edits without a problem.

191

5 To customize your theme, click **Customize** on the left under Appearance. Different templates will show you different options here. There is a link under Appearance to **Menus**, which enables you to create a custom menu.

Hot tip

Visit your public website, and then use your browser's menu to save the complete web page. This will save the HTML, images and CSS to your computer. You can then experiment with editing the CSS using your tool of choice. You can preview the results on your saved page, too. When you're ready, copy and paste the CSS into WordPress.

6 Click **Theme File Editor** (under Appearance on the left), and you can edit the CSS and PHP templates.

Adding pages

WordPress lets you add pages to your website. Typically, these pages contain information that will be updated relatively infrequently, such as the About Us section. Pages are added to your navbar.

Hot tip

You can make a page appear underneath another page in the navigation. For example, you might add Contact Us under About Us. To specify which page you would like the page you're editing to be under, click **Page** on the right and then open the **Page Attributes** pane. Give your page a parent in the **Page Attributes** pane. Use the **Order number** option to change the order of the links on the navbar.

1. Log in to WordPress and click **Pages** on the left. By default, you have a sample page. You can see any other pages you have added here, and can click a page title to edit that page. Click the **Add New** button.

2. Enter your page title in the first box, where it says **Add Title**. This will be used as the title of the link to this page from the navbar, so keep it short and meaningful – for example: About Us, The Team, Our Offices.

3. Use the WordPress Block Editor to add your page content. Each part of your content (like a paragraph or an image) is a block. If you want to add a paragraph, start typing it. Otherwise, type / to open the menu to add an image, heading, list or other popular block. You can also click the + sign in the top left to open a menu of all blocks on the left, as shown below. When you click a block or select text in it, formatting options appear in a floating menu.

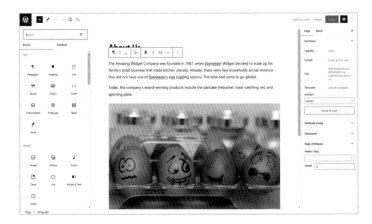

4. To save your page, click **Save Draft** on the right. Click the **Preview** button to view your page. When you're happy, click the **Publish** or **Update** button.

Adding posts

Posts are typically used for content you intend to update regularly. For example, each news story or new blog entry will be a post. Individual posts aren't added to the navbar, but posts are dated and visitors can browse them by month or post category.

There are similarities in the way that you manage pages and posts, but there are some differences, too.

Here's how to add a post:

1 Log in to WordPress and click **Posts** on the left. You'll see a list of posts and, as with pages, you can edit a post by clicking its title. Click **Add New** to create a new post.

2 The title won't be used on the navbar, so you can afford to make it more descriptive.

3 Add your article in the same way as you do for pages, building it up from blocks of content.

4 On the right, click **Post**, and you can add categories for your posts. This is an important navigational tool because it organizes posts into groups people can easily browse. A post can appear in more than one category. For optimal usability, limit your site to a small selection of categories.

5 Add tags to your posts on the right. These are short descriptive keywords or phrases used by visitors to find related posts. Tag classification is looser than a category. An article might be in the "dogs" category if it's all about dogs. It might have the tag "dogs" even if they are just mentioned in passing.

6 You can save a draft while you work. When you've finished, click the **Preview** button to proofread your post before it's published to the world.

7 Click **Publish** when it's ready. WordPress will make it the first post on your site, and add it to your archives, category and tag navigation automatically.

Hot tip

In the **Post** menu on the right, you can also add a featured image that will be used in some themes to represent your article on your homepage and in your blog archive.

Managing comments

WordPress enables you to accept comments on your posts and pages, which can be a valuable way to get feedback from your audience. You need to review and approve comments to ensure your site doesn't get bogged down in unwanted adverts (spam).

1 When you log in to your WordPress Dashboard, you'll see how many comments are awaiting approval on the navbar. Click **Comments** to review them.

2 Read the comments. When you hover the mouse over a comment, links appear to approve the comment or move it to the Spam or Trash folders. Use these links to approve or delete comments, if you only have a few. You can also edit comments, but that's rarely used. If you do edit someone's comment, make clear what you've changed so that you don't misrepresent them.

3 If you have lots of comments to process, check the box beside any you want to approve. Then, click the **Bulk Actions** menu and choose **Approve**. Click **Apply** to approve all checked comments. Use a similar process (with a different bulk action) to move a group of comments to Spam or Trash.

Hot tip

People expect permission to leave comments on posts (which are typically led by opinion or news), but not on pages (which are usually about you). It's probably not appropriate to invite public comments on your terms and conditions, for example. When editing a page or post, select **Post** on the right and then choose **Discussion**. You can then allow or disable comments.

Hot tip

Check the Spam folder from time to time, in case WordPress has classified a genuine comment as junk by mistake.

12 Testing and launching

Once your site has been designed, you need to test that it works as expected and is easy to use before you publish it on your server.

Beware

After spending perhaps months building a site, you might be impatient to launch it. Make sure you plan enough time to test properly before your launch, though. First impressions count.

Hot tip

Websites sometimes do a beta launch, which means they invite people to use the site, on the understanding that there might be the odd bug because it's not yet complete. You can get away with this if your website is innovatively interactive. If you're just publishing content or using well-tried methods of interaction (such as visitor reviews and comments), this smacks of a lack of testing and/ or confidence.

When is it ready to launch?

Building a successful website is rarely a one-off construction job. If it's a business site, you'll want to extend it with new products and services as the business develops. If it's a personal site, you'll want to add new stories, photos or music.

The beauty of the web is that it's easy to do that, but the downside is that you can get paralyzed into never launching the site, because there's always more you can do. A website that's still on your hard drive isn't really a website at all, so it's a good idea to launch early and expand it gradually, over time. There are five benefits to doing that:

- Google likes to see sites that are growing with new content. If you publish everything at one time, it will think your site is stagnant, and will prioritize more lively sites over yours.

- Search engines can start to index the early content you post, and other sites can start linking to it, so you can begin to build a rank in the search engines. This can take a long time (measured in months), so the earlier you start, the better.

- People won't spend an hour browsing your site to read everything there on their first visit, but you might convince them to visit regularly, to see the new content you've added since their last visit.

- You can refine the design of the site using feedback from visitors and analytics data.

- Whether you want your site to drive sales or build a reputation, the earlier it's live, the earlier it can start working for you.

The one caveat is that the site must offer a complete experience, even if it has fewer features than you ultimately plan to launch. Visitors get frustrated if they click on a link, wait for a web page to download, and then find that it just says "under construction" or, worse still, that the link is broken. Website visitors are impatient, and if you waste their time, they'll abandon your site and won't come back. If you haven't created a section yet, don't implement links to it yet, either. You can change any web page any time, so you can always go back and add those links later.

Before launching your site, you should test it thoroughly.

Testing your website

Testing is an important part of the website development process. If you're working with a web design firm, they might send you sections of the website to test at regular intervals. If you're building the site yourself, you'll probably develop the site iteratively, coding something, trying it in your browser, refining your design and repeating, until it's finished.

Before you launch your website, there are two different types of testing you need to perform:

- **Technical testing:** This tests whether the site works as designed. It identifies issues such as broken links and designs that do not render correctly in a particular web browser.

- **Usability testing:** This is about making sure that your site is designed intuitively so that it can be easily used.

For the best results, you should test your site early during development and test it often. Technical problems tend to be easier to fix the earlier they are identified. To fix a usability problem, you might need to redesign elements of the site or its content. If that's left to the end of the process, you'll already be too committed to the existing design, which will make it harder to justify the delay and expense caused by rework.

Testing your site offline

Most websites can be tested on a computer without uploading them to the internet. Just open the homepage in your web browser and you should be able to navigate the site. This will only work if your website does not use programs on the server, such as PHP scripts or WordPress.

You will need to reference all files in your HTML using relative paths so that they work on your hard disk. Instead of embedding the image **http://www.example.com/photos/dog.jpg**, for example, use a relative path like **photos/dog.jpg**.

You can also upload your website to the internet at a secret location (often called a staging server). Sometimes it's as simple as creating a folder on your website's intended final server and putting all your files in there. Instead of **www.example.com**, you could test your site by publishing it at **www.example.com/hidden/index.html** and then visiting that page in your browser.

Hot tip

Testing on your computer won't pick up any problems with uploading the website to the server. A common problem is case sensitivity. On your desktop, index.htm and INDEX.HTM are the same file. On the server, they might be treated as two different ones. Make sure you test your website after it goes live, too.

Beware

Putting your website into a folder you don't tell anyone about gives you some privacy, but if the test version must remain secret, you need to protect your staging server with a password. That will stop search engines stumbling across it and sending it visitors.

Technical testing

Nearly everything you need to know about technical testing is encapsulated in this short guideline: try to break your website. Do anything a visitor might, and anything else you can imagine, that might lead to unpredictable results. Be inventive. For example:

- What happens if you type nonsense into the contact form, register with an invalid email address, or submit incomplete data? Do you end up with corrupt data in your database? Also, can the form cope with foreign addresses?

- What happens if JavaScript is disabled? Can people still navigate your site and access its core content?

- Does it work on an iPad or games console? What about older desktop browsers? And current versions of Edge, Firefox, Safari, Chrome and Opera?

- Is the site fast enough when running from a server? What about if you're using a mobile device without Wi-Fi?

- Do all the links and buttons work as they should? Does the navbar look right in every section of your website?

- Can you discover any broken images?

- Does the forum work as it should? Can you add new posts and reply to others? What about the shopping cart? Or social networking integration? Or the email newsletter subscribe box?

Good testing is hard to do. It's easy to just confirm your belief that the website is working, by entering an email address with no @ symbol to check an error message is shown, or to enter a valid email address to confirm that it is accepted without triggering any alerts. The difficult bit is to test for what happens if the address is invalid in a way you haven't checked for in your validation code (such as a mistyped domain extension).

The goal of technical testing is not to create a perfect website (whatever that might mean). It is to give you confidence that there are no errors in how your site has been coded or configured, and that users don't have a bad experience because of technical issues, or when they make a mistake. Fix important problems, but don't get bogged down in creating an error message and response for every possible mistake. The important thing is that users can find their way back to your homepage if something goes wrong.

Generic Company Marketing Site

Thank you for your response. Your input is appreciated.

Above: I saw this message when I contacted a major music retailer. It told me that they hadn't configured their plug-in contact form from the generic message, and that nobody had ever tested that the script actually worked. I wondered what else they hadn't tested...

Usability testing

In a usability test, you ask people who aren't familiar with the website to try to use it. Here are some top tips:

1 It's best to test with people who are potential users of the website, if you can find them, but it's better to test with anyone than with nobody. Ask a friend or a colleague to give it a go. Anyone who doesn't know the site is fine.

2 Give people a task to do that matches one of the site's goals. For example, ask them to find something they want and buy it on the site. If you can give people some choice in the task, they'll be more emotionally invested in it.

3 While the test is going on, try to stay silent as much as possible. Don't tell people where the buttons are, because the idea is to see how easily they can figure it out. Don't give them too much information about the site beforehand, either. What matters is what's on screen.

4 Don't worry if the user makes a mistake, such as going to the wrong section, and is able to correct that themselves. If they can get themselves back on track, it shows the website is working.

5 You can ask the test participant to tell you about what they're doing while they do it, which might help you to understand their reasoning, and how they feel about the website when they encounter problems.

6 Prioritize those problems that are identified by several different people. You can't please everyone, so don't try to do everything that your participants suggest. In particular, bear in mind that everyone has a favorite color.

7 Test early and often. Ask people, informally, what they think of your sketches. Show them your design mock-ups and ask them to try your unstyled HTML pages, to see if the structure makes sense. If you leave all your testing to the end, it will be too late to make some key changes.

If test participants can't complete a task, they're not stupid. If they can't use your website, you need to refine its design.

After the site goes live, solicit and use feedback from your site visitors.

Large organizations invest heavily in usability testing, including using labs with one-way glass so that all the developers can watch the tests take place without scaring the participant. Otherwise, a low-cost informal test over a few sandwiches at lunchtime can still give you amazing insight.

Publishing your site by FTP

To launch your website, you need to copy the files from your computer to the hosting company's server. The method used to do this is called file transfer protocol (FTP). You need to know your FTP server address, your username, and your password. Your hosting company can tell you these.

Dedicated FTP software is available to download (some of it free, and some of it commercial). You can also use Windows Explorer for FTP transfer, like this:

Hot tip

If you use a content management system, it will publish pages to your server automatically once you've set it up.

1 Open a Windows Explorer window. You can do that by holding down the **Windows** key and pressing **E**.

2 Toward the top of the Explorer window is a long bar that contains the path for the files or drives you're looking at. Click here and type ftp:// followed by your FTP server address. For example, you might enter "ftp://example. com". When you've finished typing your FTP address, press the **Enter** key. If you've done this before, Windows shows possible options in a menu below the box as you type. If your address is shown, you can click it instead.

Don't forget

Your homepage needs to have a special filename. It's usually index.htm or index.html. Your hosting company can tell you what it should be for your server.

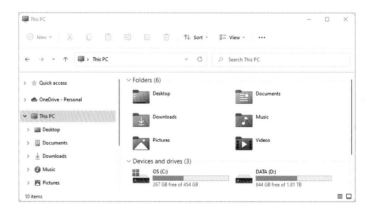

Hot tip

There are many dedicated FTP programs available. Wikipedia has an overview at **https:// en.wikipedia.org/ wiki/Comparison_of_ FTP_client_software**. Some website editors, including Dreamweaver, include a facility to upload files to your server.

3 Enter your username and password into the box. You can save your password so that you don't have to enter it next time. Click the **Log On** button.

4 Your website will open in a Windows Explorer window. Depending on how your server is set up, you might see a number of different folders. You need to find the folder that contains your public website. For my server, I double-click the public folder and then double-click the www folder. Your hosting company can tell you which folder you need to upload your files into.

5 Open a new Windows Explorer window containing your website files on your computer.

6 You can now use drag and drop to copy files and folders from your computer to your server, in the same way as you copy files between folders on your computer. Start by selecting the files you want to copy. You can select all files in a folder by holding down the **Ctrl** key and pressing **A**.

7 Click on the selected files, move your mouse pointer to the server folder, and then release the mouse button. Windows will start to copy your files across. How long this takes depends on how fast your internet connection is, and the total size of the files you are copying. Don't forget to copy across all associated files, including images and style sheets, which might be in different folders from your HTML files.

8 Once your files have uploaded, test your site works by going to your internet browser and typing in your domain name. If you see your homepage, it's working!

9 Browse around your website to check for any files that are missing or not working correctly. You can use the W3C Link Checker tool to automatically check for broken links. Visit **https://validator.w3.org/checklink** and enter your starting page's URL. Select the box to check linked documents recursively, which will check the links on linked pages too. Tell it how many levels deep you want it to check, and click **Check**.

Don't delete any files or folders that your hosting company puts on your server, unless you understand what they do and know that removing them won't interfere with your website's operation.

201

Take special care not to overwrite the latest version on your PC with an old version from the server. To avoid confusion when copying from your PC to your server, I suggest you always arrange your PC window on the left and your server window on the right.

Updating your website

After your website has been uploaded to your server, you can easily make changes in the future. You don't have to re-upload the entire website.

To modify the content of a particular web page, just edit its file on your computer. You can then upload that web page to your server and replace the old file there. If you want to add new images or web pages, you'll need to upload the files for those, and will probably need to replace some existing files to incorporate links to the new content.

Updating the look and feel

If you've designed your site using CSS (see Chapter 7), it should be easy to update the look and feel of your website by just uploading a new style sheet. When you replace a style sheet on your server, it will take effect for all the pages that use it (as long as the old style sheet isn't cached in the visitor's browser). You could dramatically transform the layout of your entire site by changing just one file on the server.

Having a fallback plan

Sometimes changes don't go quite as expected. Your site might use features that can't be tested on your computer so that, for example, the style sheet looks messy on your real site when it goes live. It's a good idea to keep a copy of the previous working version of any file you're replacing. If you can't fix any problems quickly, you can then revert to the previous version.

You can keep this copy on your computer, or you can keep it on your web server. Before you upload a new version of main.css, for example, you could rename the existing version on your server to safe-main.css. If the new file doesn't work, delete it and rename safe-main.css back to main.css to restore the previous version.

When you are using Windows Explorer for FTP, you can rename or delete a file by right-clicking on it.

Avoiding content sprawl

As you add new sections to your website, keep an eye on folder structure. Your site will be easier to maintain if you organize pages that belong to the same section in a folder. If you keep adding content at the top level of the site (that is, outside of any folders), it will become difficult to find the files you need for maintenance.

Hot tip

After uploading a new file, test that web page in your browser to make sure it's worked okay. If you don't see a change, clear your browser cache and then try again.

Hot tip

If you're using a website editor, it will usually be able to update individual files for you on the server.

Don't forget

You can incorporate a blog in your website to enable you to easily add news stories or other updates later.

13 Promoting your website

Getting people to visit your website is essential for making it successful. You can use SEO techniques to help search engines to index and rank your website.

Introducing search results

For most websites, search engines are an essential source of visitors. They're the first place people go when they're looking for something specific online, and if that's something your website can offer them, you want the search engines to recommend your website. Without a good ranking in search engine results, your website can be close to invisible.

In this chapter, I'll share some key ideas that will help your site perform well in search engine results. First, you need to have an understanding of how search engines work and how people use them to find websites.

There are two parts to the Google search engine results:

- Adverts are triggered by the keywords you entered into the search engine. They can appear as the first search results, in a sidebar on the right, and at the bottom of the search results. It's not always obvious they're adverts. You can bid to place your adverts using Google Ads.

- The rest of the page contains what are often called organic search results. These are Google's best guess at giving you links to the information you're searching for. Sometimes, they include images, videos or news stories. Google knows about over a trillion web pages, and the organic results are picked from these, based on Google's assessment of how well they match what you're looking for. No money changes hands, and you can't buy your way to the top of the organic search results. You can influence them, though, through careful design of your website and its content.

The practice of tweaking your website to help its content rank well in organic search results is called search engine optimization (SEO).

There are some SEO techniques that are based on tricking search engines or exploiting flaws in them. These "black hat SEO" techniques risk your website being banned altogether.

Microsoft's search engine Bing (www.bing.com) and Yahoo! (www.yahoo.com) use a similar results format to Google.

How people search

If somebody asked you to find a cheap flight to Spain, you probably wouldn't just type "flights" into Google. For most queries, people type in a few words so that they can more easily find what they're looking for, such as "cheap flights Spain". This is known as a key phrase.

Google will typically return millions of results, and tell you how many it's found at the top of the screen. At the bottom of the screen, there are controls for moving through the pages of results:

In practice, people rarely make it past the first few pages. If your site is ranked on page three of the search engine results, you might as well not be there at all.

Many people won't even make it to page two. Instead, they will refine their search query by adding more words to it and searching again, making the search engine work smarter for them, instead of trawling through pages of semi-relevant results. These additional words are called "qualifiers".

The kinds of words they add include:

- Adjectives that better describe what they want.

- Brand names for companies or products they especially want.

- Location details, such as a country, town or city.

- Details of a product type, such as "student discount flights".

- A verb indicating their intended action, such as "book flights" or "compare flights".

If you can use the same words on your website that people use to search, and put them in the right place on your site, you'll make it easy for Google to recommend your site when it thinks it might be the best result. Before you can do that, you need to research which words people are actually using.

Beware

Not all search phrases deliver equally valuable visitors. Those searching for "cheap" will be highly price-sensitive, and so will be easily swayed by a rival's cheaper price. Those searching using words like "buy" are closer to making a purchase, and so might be more valuable to you.

Hot tip

People don't search for marketing guff. They search for products, places, people, benefits, content and help (among other things). Think like a customer when you research your keywords.

Researching key phrases

The Google Ads Keyword Planner shares some of Google's intelligence about the words and phrases that people use to search.

The tool is designed for Ads customers so that they can optimize their paid-for listings. But it's free to use, and the results are equally applicable to organic SEO.

Don't forget

You will probably have different key phrases and qualifiers for the different pages on your website.

1 Go to **https://ads.google.com/aw/keywordplanner/home**
Log in to your Google account, or create one.

2 Click **Discover new keywords**.

3 You can enter some keywords to start with, and add your website address to filter out irrelevant keyword ideas. Alternatively, you can start with a website, and Google will analyze the site to suggest relevant keywords. That site could be yours, or a competitor's. Use the tabs to switch between starting with keywords and a website.

Hot tip

Google Insights for Search (**https://trends.google.com/trends**) shows you the most popular search terms in different categories, enables you to compare how popular search terms are in different countries and towns, and shows you seasonal variations.

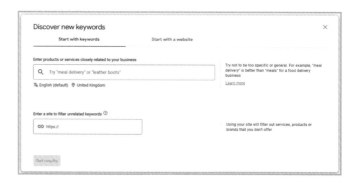

4 Click the **Get results** button.

5 Click the tab to view the keyword ideas.

6 The web page shows a table of suggested keywords. You can click one of the columns to sort the results by it.

Hot tip

If a key phrase has a lot of competition, it might not be worth trying to compete on it. It's better to identify niche phrases you can dominate than to languish on page 20 of the search results for a highly popular phrase.

7 The Avg. monthly searches column tells you how many times a particular keyword is used. Google only gives you broad ranges to work with here, but you can see which keywords are the most popular.

8 The Competition column shows you how heavily contested these words or phrases are for advertising. It doesn't affect organic search results, but it is a good indication of how hard it might be to rank for a particular word or phrase.

9 Use the Refine keywords option to remove categories of keywords that aren't relevant to your website.

10 Make a note of phrases that people frequently use to find your kind of content, but exclude any that are obviously too unspecific for your site to satisfy.

Hot tip

Try searching for things on Google to see which terms it recommends as you type. Many people will select one of these, even if they intended to type something else.

Where to put search terms

Following keyword research and brainstorming, you should have a number of key phrases that apply across your site, and between five and ten qualifiers that might be used to fine-tune results.

You might have keywords and key phrases that apply to different pages on your website. For example, you might have search terms that are specific to different product pages (perhaps even model numbers), as well as broader terms that you would like your homepage to rank against (such as "buy camera"). Search engines are not case-sensitive, so don't worry about whether the terms appear in upper- or lowercase in your web pages.

Using search terms in headlines
If your website is correctly marked up using HTML, search engines can understand which bits of the page are headlines and will give the words in them more weight. Use your search terms in your headings, and make sure that your headings are correctly marked up using heading tags like <h1> (see Chapter 6).

Using search terms in your articles
You also need to scatter your search terms liberally throughout the main content of your web pages. Your primary key phrases should be used without any words splitting them up. You can distribute your qualifiers throughout the article, and should use variations wherever possible. For example, if you have an article about singing, use variants such as sing, sung, sang, sings, and singing.

Using search terms in your link text
The words in a text link are understood by Google to be a description of the page linked to. This applies even if the link is between two pages on your own website. It's a good idea to include a key phrase in your internal links, wherever possible.

Using search terms in your page title
There is an HTML tag that is used to mark up the title of a web page. This title doesn't appear as part of the web page content (unlike your headings), but it is shown in the title bar at the top of the browser window. It's also used as the bookmark name when somebody adds a page to their favorites.

Google uses the title tag as the text for its link to your site in its search engine results pages. A good title can encourage people to click through to your site.

You add your title between <title> and </title> tags in the header of your HTML document. You should keep your title tag to about 60 characters (including spaces), and include one of your most important key phrases. Make sure the title encourages users to click the search result, and that each page has a unique title.

Using search terms in your description

You can feed search engines a description of your site to use in their search engine results, too. You use what's called a meta tag in your web page, which includes information about the page that doesn't normally appear in the web page content.

In your description meta tag, you have about 120 characters to sell the benefits of your site, and encourage people to visit. Think back to the differentiators you created when planning your website. They will help you to write a description that sells the unique benefits of your website. Give each page a unique description, and make it specific to the web page. Use one of your keywords or key phrases in your description.

Here's how you use the description meta tag:

```
<meta name="description" content="Description here">
```

How Google displays your page in search results

Below you can see example HTML from a web page that has a title tag and description meta tag. This is just an excerpt: there would typically be other code between the <head> and </head> tags too. The screengrab shows what that page looks like in Google's search engine results:

```
<head>
<title>Friends of the Earth | Home</title>
<meta name="description" content="Friends of the Earth
is an environmental campaigning community dedicated
to the wellbeing and protection of the natural world
and everyone in it.">
</head>
```

---

https://friendsoftheearth.uk :

Friends of the Earth | Home

Friends of the Earth is an **environmental** campaigning community dedicated to the wellbeing and protection of the natural world and everyone in it.

Planning and environmental law · About us · Make a donation today · Our history

---

When Google shows search results, it puts the terms the user searched for in bold. If these terms are in your title and description, it will draw the eye and encourage people to visit your site.

Google doesn't always use your suggested description. Sometimes it creates its own description for the search results, based on your page content.

7 top tips for SEO

Hot tip

The best way to get links is to create fantastic content that people want to link to.

Beware

A link from one web page to another is usually seen by search engines as an endorsement of it, but sites can include a code in the link to say that it shouldn't be. This is typically used in blog comments and other places where people can submit their own links unchecked. Mark up any links you don't want to endorse with the nofollow attribute:

```
<a href="http://
www.example.com"
rel="nofollow">Link
text</a>
```

1 One of the most influential factors for ranking your website is the number of links it has coming into it, and where those links come from. One-way links to your site (that is, links you don't reciprocate) are rated as more important, but it's still a good idea to exchange links with business partners, and others you trust. Don't swap links with spammy sites: if you get into a bad link neighborhood, Google might penalize you. Only link to sites you're happy to recommend.

2 If you can get others to link to you, try to get them to use one of your desired search terms in their link text.

3 Avoid having content in your site that is duplicated, either elsewhere on your site or on another site.

4 Use descriptive names for the folders on your site and your filenames. If your editor automatically creates pages with names like Page1.htm, change them to more descriptive names, such as buying-cameras.htm. Use a hyphen to separate any words in your file or folder names, and try to use some of your search terms here, too.

5 Make sure every page on your website can be reached through a simple HTML link. You can consider having a sitemap page that links to every other page, to make it easy for search engines to find all your web pages. Beware of using JavaScript for navigation, because search engines might struggle to follow it.

6 Update your site regularly. Google likes to see a site that is being regularly refreshed with new content. Having a blog can help.

7 Google Search Console (**https://search.google.com/search-console/about**) gives you insight into how your page is performing in search engines. It will also tell you if Google has spotted any technical issues that negatively affect your visitors' experience.

Submitting your website

Search engines use programs called spiders to crawl the web: the program looks at a web page, follows the links in it, looks at that web page, and keeps crawling deeper into the web.

If you have links coming in to your website, search engines should be able to discover it naturally. However, you can help them to discover your website by submitting it to them directly.

1 Register for Google Search Console (**https://search.google.com/search-console/about**).

2 You will need to verify your ownership of your website. You can do this by uploading a special file to your site or adding an HTML tag to a page on your site, among other methods.

3 Select **URL inspection** on the navbar on the left.

4 Enter your website address in the bar at the top of the window. You can use this feature to inspect any URL on your website, but if you're submitting it for the first time, start with your homepage.

> Q Inspect any URL in 'https://www.sean.co.uk/'

5 Google tells you if your web page is not indexed. Click the link to request indexing, and your page will be queued up for a visit by the Googlebot web crawler.

> **ⓘ URL is not on Google**
> This page is not indexed. Pages that aren't indexed can't be served on Google. See the details below to learn why it wasn't indexed. Learn more
>
> VIEW CRAWLED PAGE   Page changed? **REQUEST INDEXING**

6 Google says it can take at least a week for your site to be indexed. Use **URL inspection** in Google Search Console again to check whether your page has been indexed.

For these tips to work, you should ideally have a memorable domain name, and be able to tell people about a clear benefit for them of visiting your website. You might be able to offer out-of-hours support, discounts, online ordering or exclusive content, for example.

Links aren't just beneficial for search engine rankings. A link in a prominent position on a busy website can bring you lots of visitors. The best link relationships come when somebody has a genuine desire to recommend your website, so focus on creating great content and building solid relationships, rather than begging strangers for links.

More promotion tips

It's not just about SEO and advertising. There are many other ways and places you could promote your site. You've probably thought of some already, but here are a few suggestions:

- **In your business.** Include your website address on your business cards, letters, vans, carrier bags, and receipts. Add a plug for your website to your email signature so that a short advert goes out with every email you send.

- **Offline advertisements.** Buy adverts in magazines, shop windows or wherever else your potential visitors might be.

- **Online advertisements.** You can bid for placement in search engine results using Google Ads (**https://adwords.google.com**) or Bing's advertising system (**https://about.ads.microsoft.com/**). Set a daily budget limit! Both sites also operate a partner network that you can advertise across. If you know of a website that reaches your target audience, you might be able to advertise on it, too, if you contact it directly.

- **Network.** Participate in forums, social networks, and blog commenting to connect with others who might like your website content. You can't just turn up and start advertising, but if you become a valued member of the community, people will notice you and your profile with a link to your website.

- **Create an affiliate program.** Affiliate programs enable you to pay websites for sending you paying customers. Amazon has pioneered this model with its Associates program, which pays websites a commission on any sales referred through a link. Several intermediaries exist to help you set up your affiliate program, including Tradedoubler (**www.tradedoubler.com**) and Commission Junction (**www.cj.com**).

- **Create an email newsletter.** Mailchimp (**www.mailchimp.com**) is an affordable system for managing lists and sending emails. It provides a subscription form for your website. A newsletter helps you to build a relationship with your website visitors and to convert them into customers.

- **Add a sharing button.** Help visitors to recommend your site on their social networks. AddThis (**www.addthis.com**) provides code you can add to your site to help readers post your link on their favorite social networks.

(14) Measuring success

Gather data about website visitors and how they use your site to help evolve your website design and content.

Right: The SiteAnalytics tool provided by Ionos for its hosting clients includes reports showing how many visits the site gets from robots, including search engine robots.

Measuring visitor interaction

There are two different approaches you can use to measure how people use your website. One uses the server's record of the files it sent out (the server log), and the other uses JavaScript to identify human visitors.

Both typically provide reports through a web interface, so you don't need to install any software. Neither approach is perfect, so it's best to use both together.

Using server logs

Your hosting company will usually provide statistics to you, which are based on your server logs. You may also be able to download the raw logs and analyze them using your choice of software.

The advantage of using server logs is that they can tell you which search engine spiders are visiting your site and what errors occurred (such as missing pages). You can also measure downloads of non-HTML files, such as PDF files or MP3s, relatively accurately. Server logs cannot be blocked by visitors, and include traffic on devices with JavaScript disabled.

The disadvantage of using server logs is that they have no insight into what people actually do. The reporting tools make some clever guesses, but the tools often can't tell the difference between one long visit and two short ones. Your server logs will include a lot of web spider traffic, inflating some of the headline metrics.

If somebody views a page from their browser's cache or from their Internet Service Provider's (ISP's) cache, it won't show up in your stats at all. Some internet connections might look like one person in your logs, but could actually represent many hundreds or thousands of people.

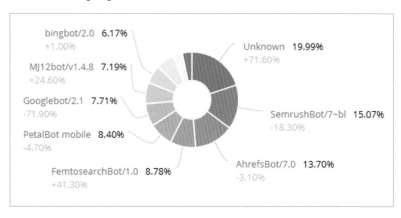

bingbot/2.0 **6.17%**
+1.00%

MJ12bot/v1.4.8 **7.19%**
+24.60%

Googlebot/2.1 **7.71%**
-71.90%

PetalBot mobile **8.40%**
-4.70%

FemtosearchBot/1.0 **8.78%**
+41.30%

Unknown **19.99%**
+71.60%

SemrushBot/7-bl **15.07%**
-18.30%

AhrefsBot/7.0 **13.70%**
-3.10%

Using JavaScript tags

To get around the limitations of server log analysis, web analytics solutions were invented that use JavaScript. Each web page has a small snippet of JavaScript code added into it, which is executed whenever the web page is loaded into the browser.

That code then tracks what visitors do on the web page, measuring the length of their visit and the path they take through the website. Web analytics solutions using JavaScript can even measure repeated views of web pages stored in a cache.

Although this provides much richer and more human data than server log analysis, it has its drawbacks. 37% of web users worldwide install ad-blocker extensions to remove ads from web pages they visit (source: GWI, Q3 2021). These extensions also block web analytics software, so your analytics may be significantly under-reporting your visitors.

The analytics code you add to your website will have a small impact on its download time. The biggest challenge is that you have to add the tag to every page on your website. Some HTML editors will enable you to easily modify all your web pages at once, using templates or a site-wide search and replace. If your site uses a content management system, you can usually add the tag to your page template once.

There are lots of analytics solutions available. Google Analytics (**www.google.com/analytics**) is one of the most popular, and it's free, so it's well worth trying it out. Google Analytics uses graphs, maps and pie charts to help you identify trends and demographics. You can drill down into the numbers for more detail.

Microsoft Clarity (**https://clarity.microsoft.com**) is another free analytics tool. One of its best features enables you to play back recordings of visitor activity on your web pages. You can see when visitors scroll and where they click or tap.

Web analytics software uses cookies, which are small text files that the browser can store on the visitor's device. Some people delete their cookies regularly, which will stop the analytics software identifying those repeat visitors.

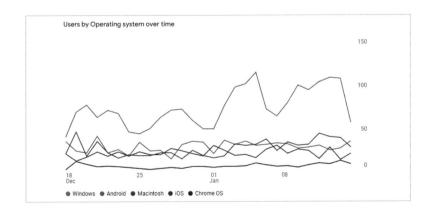

Left: Google Analytics uses graphs to make it easy to understand trends in visitor demographics and the technologies used by site visitors.

Often, the trends in the numbers are more useful than the absolute values. Don't fixate on your number of visitors, but do worry about whether they go up or down in the medium term. Expect to see fluctuations from month to month.

Don't forget to check your stats from time to time, to see how your site is performing. It's easy to forget, so why not put it in your diary for the end of each month?

The landing and exit pages are the pages where people arrive at and depart from your website.

What the numbers mean

People talk in hushed tones about "analysis paralysis": having so much data you don't know where to start. Analytics software can seem a bit daunting at first, but once you understand what the data means, you can easily focus on the most useful bits.

This is what the metrics represent:

- **Hits.** You might see this in your server log stats, but you should largely ignore it. Every file download is a hit, so a web page with a style sheet and three pictures might be five hits. It tells you nothing about human behavior.

- **Bandwidth.** The total size of all the files downloaded by your visitors and spiders. Pay attention to your bandwidth if your hosting package has a limit. (Most don't now.)

- **Unique visitors.** The number of different people who visited your website. The software is fooled by people who use multiple browsers or computers, and by people who share a browser. But this metric remains the best indication of how many individuals visited your site.

- **Number of sessions or visits.** The number of different occasions on which people visited your site. This will include the total number of visits by regular visitors, as well as one-off visits by others.

- **Pages or page views.** The number of different web pages that were viewed.

- **Views/user.** The average number of pages viewed per visitor is a good way to measure how engaged your visitors are.

- **Average engagement time.** In Google Analytics, this is how long users were active on the site on average.

- **Bounce rate.** The percentage of people who arrived at one page and left your site at that same page. A high bounce rate might reflect poor navigation between pages on your site, might show that people didn't find what they wanted on your site, or might be a good thing if people are clicking on adverts to leave and you're being paid for that click.

- **New users.** The percentage of people visiting the site that the analytics package doesn't recognize from a previous visit.

Other important metrics

The number of visitors on a website and how long they spend there are important metrics, but they're rarely an indicator of whether the site is meeting its objectives or not. Few sites are built purely to be looked at.

Think back to the purpose of your site, which you defined when you were planning it. What is the best way to benchmark your success? Ideally, you will have defined this at the start of the project, too. For example:

- If you want to improve customer service, measure how the website is affecting the number of returns, complaints or phone calls you receive. Survey customers to see whether they are more satisfied now than they were before.

- To see how your website is affecting your reputation, look at how many people link to your website and what they write about it. Research how often your web pages are recommended on social media sites.

- If you aim to sell, measure your total sales volume, value of sales per customer and number of customers. Consider any offline sales that are influenced by the website, where appropriate, too.

- Where it's important to build relationships, look at the number of email newsletter subscribers, registered members or social media followers you have.

- If you want to create a community or learn from your audience, then consider how many comments and forum postings your site attracts, and the quality of that user-generated content.

You might need to introduce sophisticated tracking systems in your business to gather some of the information you need. For example, when customers phone up, ask them where they found your number and keep a record of it. If customers call up to complain, find out whether the website failed them or whether they didn't think to go there.

Often, you can't easily tell whether your site is meeting its goals or not. It all depends on how visitors react to it. The only sure way to find that out is to ask them.

Hot tip

If you use bit.ly (https://bit.ly) to create a shortened version of a link, bit.ly will count each time your link is clicked. You can use this to measure the effectiveness of particular link placements. Search engines might not give you credit for links via bit.ly, though, so use it for isolated tests.

Creating a survey

The numbers are good for telling you what people do on your website, but they don't tell you much about why, or about how your visitors feel about your website experience. Find out with a quick survey from SurveyMonkey (**www.surveymonkey.com**). Here's how to create one:

Don't give people too many options, or ask them to grade things too finely. Don't add too many questions, either. If the survey is too hard to complete, people won't bother.

1 Create an account for SurveyMonkey, if you don't already have one, or log in if you do. Click the button at the top to create a survey. Choose to start with a blank survey.

2 Give it a name. Choose a category, choose to use your own contacts and click **Create Survey**.

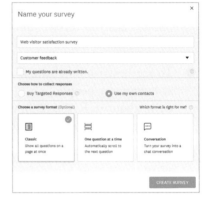

3 Enter your first question. You can choose from a number of question formats, including multiple choice, comment boxes and star ratings. The customization options you have will depend on the question you're asking. For a multiple-choice question, you can use the menu to set up a scale of responses easily.

Hot tip

People don't like sharing personal information, so don't ask for too much. Make it clear that you want to learn how to help your visitors, and are not gathering information for marketing purposes.

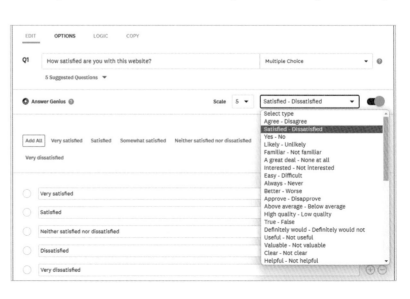

4 Click **Next Question** to add another question. You can keep adding questions until you've finished. You can also add pages to the survey.

5 When you've finished adding questions, click the **Done** button to edit the button. This is the button that users will use to submit their survey. You can change its name.

6 Click the **Save** button at the bottom.

7 When you've finished, click the **Next** button at the top to preview your survey.

8 Click the **Collect Responses** button. Select the option to "send surveys your way". Choose to share a survey link. Copy the link, and add it to your website. You'll need to paste it into an HTML link tag (see Chapter 6). When users follow the link, they will be taken to the SurveyMonkey site to complete your survey. There is a premium option to embed the survey within your website.

9 Test the survey works and publish your web page. To get your data, log in to your account.

You can find code examples, and other supporting resources at www.ineasysteps.com or on the author's website, at www.sean.co.uk

If you enjoyed this book, please blog about it or write a review of it on your favorite online store. Thank you!

Enabling evolution

Your analytics data is as close as you can get to looking over your visitors' shoulders while they visit your website. It's extremely valuable information, but only if you use it. Operating a website should be an iterative process, where you use what you learn to continuously refine your design and content.

When you know which pages and stories people are most interested in, and those they tend to ignore, you can take the guesswork out of creating new content that meets their needs.

Your analytics and survey data tell you which devices, browsers and screen resolutions people will use to view your website so that you can ensure your site offers a good experience to your visitors.

As well as using your data to refine your design, you can use it to refine your online strategy. Imagine you're running a shop and it's not selling as much as you want it to. By looking at your data, you can see whether you have an empty shop, or whether you have lots of visitors leaving empty-handed. If you don't have enough visitors, web promotion is your priority. If you have plenty of people browsing, look at how you can improve your conversion of visitors into sales. What stops people ordering?

Using a combination of web analytics, surveys and usability testing, you can ensure that you're not making changes for the sake of it, and that your website continuously evolves to better achieve the purpose you defined at the start of this book.

Acknowledgments

Many thanks to Karen McManus, Leo McManus, and Sevanti and Ruth at In Easy Steps. Refreshable Braille display photo by Sebastien Delorme; dice image by Ed Sanders, both at Wikimedia Commons CC BY-SA 3.0. Thanks to Tengyart, Marcel Eberle, Possessed Photography, Tony Hand, David Pisnoy, Anne Nygard, Clem Onojeghuo, Maximalfocus, and Kanan Khasmammadov, all at Unsplash.com, for images used in examples.

About the author

Sean McManus is a copywriter and journalist specializing in technology. His other books include *100 Top Tips: Microsoft Excel*, *Scratch Programming in easy steps*, *Cool Scratch Projects in easy steps*, *Coder Academy* and *Mission Python*. Get free chapters and bonus resources at **www.sean.co.uk**

Index